The
CHINESE
SHAR PEI
Today

JULIETTE CUNLIFFE

HOWELL
BOOK HOUSE

New York

HOWELL BOOK HOUSE
A Prentice Hall Macmillan Company
15 Columbus Circle
New York, NY 10023

MACMILLAN is a registered trademark of Macmillan, Inc.

Library of Congress Cataloging-in-Publication data

the chinese shar pei today / juliette cunliffe

Library of Congress catalogue card number: 94–73810
ISBN 0–87605–095–X

Manufactured in Singapore

10 9 8 7 6 5 4 3 2 1

CONTENTS

PREFACE

The Shar Pei is an incredible breed, one which becomes more and more intriguing the more one delves into its history, development and character, not to mention its looks.

It has many enthusiasts throughout the world and I hope that those who are genuinely dedicated to the Shar Pei can strive to work, in harmony with one another, for the benefit of the breed's future. Any relatively 'new' breed encounters troubles along the way, but it behoves us all to remember that it is the betterment of the dog which must always remain uppermost in our minds.

Many people have helped me by providing information for this book, and to them I extend my warmest gratitude. Firstly I must thank Carole Lilley for her excellent drawings. How lucky I am to have found such a talented artist who is also thoroughly conversant with the breed. Such a find is like gold-dust! Bill Lilley has been kind enough to provide me with a multitude of excellent photographs and, I know, has gently tried to prod others into similar action. Both Carole and Bill have shared with me much other information and have been thoroughly supportive in the compilation of this book.

Peter Embling, Susan Stead, Dulcie Ligget, Wendy Coates and Dawne Bullen have all provided information which has been of assistance, as has Linda Rupniak, who has looked deeply into the problems of amyloidosis and the use of natural remedies. I am grateful to Bob Brampton for sharing with me his fascinating experiences of judging Shar Pei in the Far East.

Letters, faxes and telephone calls have brought me into close contact with Shar Pei breeders and enthusiasts in the USA and, amongst the many people there to whom I owe my thanks, are Tibetan Spaniel owner and author, Susan Miccio, for pointing me in the right direction, Mary Ellen Tarman, Betsy Davison, Colleen Kehe, Kathy Kamakeeaina and Pat Gear. Thanks also to the Canadian Kennel Club.

On the subject of Kennel Clubs, yet again I owe my heartfelt thanks to Teresa Slowik and Elaine Camroux of the English Kennel Club's Library for their kind help; they must be two of the luckiest people in the world to be surrounded by such a veritable wealth of information.

Finally, my thanks to you for reading this book: I hope its content will help you to understand more about the Shar Pei.

JULIETTE CUNLIFFE

Chapter One

HISTORY OF THE BREED

As a writer who is thoroughly absorbed in the history and development of dogs, I would love to be able to open this chapter with clear-cut facts about the Shar Pei's evolution through the centuries. Alas, this is not possible, as little has been authentically documented, and it is not always easy to separate fact from fiction.

There have been many periods during China's long history when its people were interested in dog breeding, but the dogs were not kept only as companions. They also assisted man in hunting, and the dogs themselves were often used to provide meat, pelts and leather. Unfortunately, a great deal of material, which could have helped us in our current quest for information about the origin of China's canine population, was destroyed by the Emperor Ch'in Shih around 255 BC. Records towards the end of the first century AD become a little more specific in relation to dogs, but the Chinese language makes abundant use of flowery allegory and comparisons, so it is sometimes difficult to be sure of precise interpretations.

What I should like to do, therefore, is to set down the theories which have evolved about the Shar Pei over the years so that, in the fullness of time, people will be able to refer back to this chapter and decide for themselves which of the history recorded here has been proved to have sound foundation.

HAN DYNASTY
It is said that the history of the breed can be traced back as far as the Han Dynasty in China, which lasted from 206 BC to 220 AD, and the original fountain-head of the breed seems to have been Dah Let (Tai Leh) in Kwun Tung Province, located near Canton, in the south of China, bordering the South China Sea. There are statuettes of tomb dogs from this time and such dogs do, indeed, bear a marked resemblance to the Shar Pei. They are clay figurines, depicting short-legged, square-bodied dogs, with a curling tail and a scowling expression about the head. On vases of the Han Dynasty some sturdily built dogs are depicted, with short, erect tails and short legs; one cannot but wonder whether there may be some connection with today's Shar Pei.

The breeds from which the Shar Pei is descended are also a matter for conjecture, but it seems certain that the Chow Chow is there in the background, in part because of its blue-black tongue. It is frequently said that the Chow and the Shar Pei are the only breeds which share this feature, but there are other Asian breeds, not known in the West, which have similar pigmentation, as does the polar bear. According to W. F. Collier, in his 'Dogs of China and Japan', the extreme poverty of the people, and the consequent difficulty in maintaining food supplies, weakened races of dog and caused them to deteriorate, but throughout China he thought there was a distinct resemblance to the Chow in what he termed 'the unclassified local breeds'.

Dogs represented on Chinese pottery of the Han Dynasty.

Chinese hunter with his dog: 210 BC, Han Dynasty.

Dogs of Ancient China (left to right): Dog featured on bas relief of Hsiad T'ang Shan; Greyhound of the Han Dynasty, engraving from an ancient Chinese encyclopaedia.

Another breed which is there in the Shar Pei's background is the Tibetan Mastiff, and maybe some others of the Molosser (Mastiff) breeds. During part of the Han Dynasty the Roman Empire was rapidly expanding and, around 200 BC, trade was opened up by the overland caravan route across Central Asia. A variety of merchandise frequently made the passage from the Roman Empire to the northern part of China, to be bartered for silk as well as other items, but still the south was barely civilised. It is not inconceivable, therefore, that the large, powerful dogs used by the Romans in their fighting arenas found their way to China.

THEORIES ABOUT THE SHAR PEI
There is a theory that the profusion of skin on the Shar Pei came about because the dog was bred down in size and, to substantiate this, the Orthopaedic Foundation for Animals classifies it as a giant breed, due to the rapid growth of the Shar Pei from puppy to adulthood. It is said, too, that the Pyrenean Mountain Dog may also have played a part in the development of the breed, because double dewclaws still appear on some Shar Pei. However, Pyreneans are not the only dogs to have double dewclaws.

It appears that, during the Han Dynasty, the Shar Pei, or one of its close ancestors such as the 'Dah-Let Fighting Dog', was used for the purposes of fighting. With powerful jaws, suitable for

LEFT: Stoneware jar of the Han Dynasty. Mount Trust Collection of Chinese Art, Victoria and Albert Museum.

RIGHT: Terra-cotta tombstone from the Han Dynasty.

grasping an opponent, and a stiff coat which would have been uncomfortable for another dog to hold in its mouth, the Shar Pei would have had added advantages. The Shar Pei actually has the ability to use its coat as a defence mechanism, stiffening it still further when required, much as another breed might raise its ruff and coat along the back. The amount and flexibility of the skin would also have provided it with the facility to turn and manoeuvre, breaking the opponent's hold with relative ease during a fight. The very thick and spongy nature of the skin would have prevented damage to underlying tissue. The amount of wrinkle was also important. Too much and the skin could be torn, too little and it provided insufficient protection. Even the smallness of the ear was an asset: in some of the original Shar Pei the ear was apparently only as large as a thumb nail, just sufficient in size to cover the opening. Such an ear, set tightly to the head, provided an attacker with little to grasp.

However, although bred for the sport of fighting, the Shar Pei provided no match for some of the heavier breeds which had found their way to China around that time and, it is said, the Shar Pei was given artificial stimulants to improve its fighting performance.

Although used as a fighting dog by pirates and sailors while they passed time in the ports of the South China coast, the Shar Pei soon became a multi-purpose dog, used also for hunting and guarding the home. In China, any dog which is used to protect property is called a 'fighting dog', and so it is possible that this term was used in relation to the Shar Pei long after the breed's fighting days were over. The game which seems most usually to have been hunted by the Shar Pei in China was the wild pig, and it is doubtful whether the breed would have made a good retriever, because one of the Shar Pei's instincts is to shake anything it catches.

TROUBLED TIMES

Dog ownership in China had been at its height during the Han Dynasty, but the centuries passed and the ravages of war and famine took their toll. With the decline of the Roman Empire the original trade route was closed but another route opened as the first century AD came to an end. There was still more destruction of records during these troubled times and this is undoubtedly one of the causes of there being such a scarcity of documentary evidence. An example of this is shown by the one-eyed Emperor and scholar Yuan during the Yuan (Mongol) Dynasty (1260-1368) who, knowing that he was to be killed, set fire to every one of his 140,000 ancient books rather than let them fall into what he considered unworthy hands. He also expressly forbade the placing of

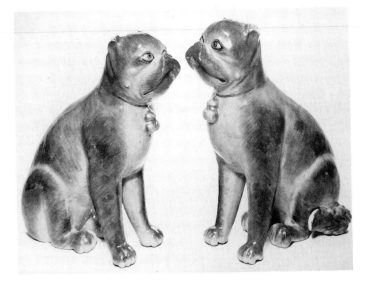

A pair of coral-coloured fighting dogs from the Ch'ien Lung period (1736-1795). Sold by auction at Sotheby's London in 1970 for the sum of £5,500.

pottery figures of dogs in his grave, as was still customary at that time. By the Ming Dynasty, which ran from 1368 until 1644, disinterest in dogs had led to a steep decline in numbers not only of the Shar Pei but of other breeds too.

TRADE BETWEEN EAST AND WEST
Apart from a period of two hundred years, beginning in the mid-fourteenth century, there have always been commercial connections between the East and the West. China opened up trade relations with Portugal in 1516, with Spain in 1575, Holland in 1604 and with England in 1637. An ambassador at the Russian Embassy in China (1662-1723) was said to be greatly interested in dogs and hounds, and some accompanied him to the East. Indeed dogs have frequently been favoured as gifts between emperors and kings.

I have been fascinated trying to locate pictures of Chinese porcelain from the Ch'ien Lung Dynasty (1736-1795). A pair of 'Fighting Dogs' was sold by Sotheby and Company, in London, in 1970, for the sum of £5,500, and another, sold by Sotheby's the following year, fetched £2,500. Measuring ten inches, the first pair was coral in colour, the bodies painted with hair and the ears small. The second pair was almost as large, again with brownish painted hair and, in both cases, the tip of the tongue protruded and was enamelled in pink. The dogs in each of the pairs wore bells around their necks, but what principally set them apart from the Shar Pei we know today, was the lack of evident wrinkle and the presence of a bushy tail. A pair, of which I have not seen photographs, was sold in the same auction house in the January of 1969.

DOGS UNDER COMMUNIST RULE
The Communists took over China in the 1940s and under the Communist regime pet dogs were considered a luxury, so heavy fines were imposed for keeping dogs of any kind. Later, Mao Tse-tung set out a decree that pets were symbols of the privileged classes and ordered a mass extermination. My interest in Asian breeds over the years has caused me to look into this matter in some depth and, without going into the gory side of the matter, what does seem certain is that, although the canine population was virtually wiped out in towns, this did not extend to all areas of

the countryside and so, thankfully, some dogs survived this wholesale massacre. By 1950 it seems that just a few small pockets of Shar Pei still survived, some of these having being smuggled into the countryside and to areas of Hong Kong, Macao and Taiwan, islands off China's mainland.

SURVIVAL AND REVIVAL

Although the Shar Pei did exist in very small numbers before the 1970s, it was in the first half of that decade that a small group of people, intent on preserving the breed, searched ardently for survivors of this fast-declining race. Two of the group were Mr C. M. Chung, who was breeding Shar Pei, and the young Mr Matgo Law, who had recently become involved with them. Though the number acquired was not large, these few dogs essentially formed the foundation of the breed we know today. The dogs discovered were taken to Hong Kong, so that a programme could be developed to re-establish the breed, for it was by then considered 'endangered'.

All available bloodlines were used, as there were so few Shar Pei from which to choose, and early matings inevitably involved the frequent use of dogs with undocumented pedigree. Inbreeding, a powerful tool if carefully used by experienced breeders, was employed, with the aim of producing dogs which resembled, as far as possible, the original type of Shar Pei. In order to re-establish the breed, efforts were concentrated on obtaining type and then soundness. Once type had been obtained, a breed standard was drawn up, so that enthusiasts could work towards this guideline of an 'ideal'.

Matgo Law is of the opinion that the Shar Pei was kept only by the lower ranks of society, by farmers and those out of work. The breed was therefore found only in the undeveloped areas and, he feels, can be traced back to the Chow Chow in its earlier form, for the Shar Pei is similar in temperament and character. Although the Shar Pei has more hind angulation than the Chow, more similar to that of the wolf and the Siberian Husky, Mr Law sees a similarity in expression. He talks of the Shar Pei's dislike of water, trying to dodge puddles following a rainfall, and considers them clean dogs, not liking to wet their beds. He recalls having seen the Shar Pei used for fighting when he was a child. The dogs had such endurance that, though their flesh may have been torn to the bone, they were still willing to fight. They were also known for their 'death grip', a pressure hold, sinking deeper into the opponent until that antagonist was dead. He believes that the blacks and the deep tan dogs were those used primarily for fighting, and that creams were seldom used for this purpose. Other breeds were crossed with the Shar Pei for the purpose of fighting, including Boxers, Bull Terriers, Staffordshire Bull Terriers and the occasional German Shepherd.

Matgo Law remembers the street traders lining the pavements of Hong Kong, with many baskets of living things, such as birds, for fighting. It was in one of these baskets that he first saw a litter of Shar Pei puppies and bought one, for 80 Hong Kong dollars. The mother had pricked ears and not an especially good head, but she had a good body. His second Shar Pei, Down-Homes Sweet Pea, was a gift from a dog fighter. Sweet Pea was described by Mr Law as being spotted, with a typical head, sunken eyes, tight ears and a sound, cobby body. From then on he looked around the farms for his next Shar Pei and his favourite line comes from Down-Homes Annie Revival, a fawn-coloured bitch. Mr Law does not consider the Shar Pei to be a good herding dog, but rather one with a strong hunting instinct, as well as being a good guard. He looks upon those with low set tails with some suspicion, possibly considering that some cross-breeding is the cause of this. He loves the breed for its wonderful character, especially the reserve with strangers which, in his opinion, suits the Chinese people very well.

Looking back, it is eminently clear that the early dogs in Hong Kong, and the first Shar Pei imported to the USA, differ from many of the Shar Pei known throughout the world today. Some people have gone so far as to say that the 'meat-mouthed' dog (see Chapter 5) did not exist before the 1960s. The dog which originally appears to have been preferred by the Chinese themselves, was lighter in bone and longer in leg than those which would take prize cards in the ring today. There was a preference for a bone mouth and, again, I would draw your attention to the chapter containing analyses of the breed standard. Suffice it to say, at this stage, that such a skull was in keeping with dogs of lighter frame. For preference, there was to be only slight wrinkling on the head, and a 'horse coat' was the one most sought after. This term stems from the Chinese horse, which has a short, bristly coat standing off from the body at an angle, so it is said, of 8%. A horse coat is prickly to touch and is the shortest of the coats found on the Shar Pei today.

There was, however, also a difference of opinion in Hong Kong as to what actually constituted a typical Shar Pei. In 1966 the Hong Kong Kennel Club discontinued registration of the Shar Pei. The reported reason for this action was that the dogs currently under application for registration no longer had the appearance or type of those registered formerly. They apparently considered that the Shar Pei which were being bred at that time had muzzles which were "more flashy", heads and bodies which were excessively wrinkled and coats which were too long and soft, or sometimes adequately short, but still soft. The suspicion was that these major differences were the result of crossbreeding.

Indeed there is still much conjecture about the history of the Shar Pei as we now know it, but I hope that the information I have pieced together will serve to assist those who continue to research the development of the breed in years to come.

Chapter Two

GETTING TO KNOW THE SHAR PEI

Being such an unusual looking breed, the Shar Pei, once seen, is unlikely to be forgotten. Though many people do not even know the breed's name, they are familiar with its looks and, once noticed by the public at large, few other breeds can have risen so quickly to fame. The Shar Pei has appeared in newspapers and magazines, on television and in advertising campaigns throughout the world and is now well known by the general public, even though many may never have seen a real, live specimen.

Fame is not always a good thing for, whilst it is of great assistance in bringing a new or rare breed to people's attention, it can also attract the attention of people who are likely to bring it into disrepute. In recent years, in the UK, the Shar Pei has received some exceptionally bad press, most of it brought about by those who have rushed into buying a dog, without having done sufficient homework about the suitability of the breed for its proposed environment. Like any breed, the Shar Pei is suitable for some owners, but not for all. There was even one newspaper report, in 1990, telling readers of a couple of pensioners in their seventies who had mistakenly bought a Meishan pig, thinking it to be a Shar Pei. Meishan pigs are bred in China, as is the Shar Pei, but there the close similarity surely ends!

LIVING WITH A SHAR PEI
The Shar Pei enjoys human contact and has been said to be extreme in developing devotion to the family, but this does not mean that the dog will necessarily be so friendly toward strangers. As is the mentality with so many of the Asian breeds, the Shar Pei will take on the responsibility of keeping the home and its owners secure, being alert to the slightest sound. If required to protect people whom the Shar Pei loves and knows well, the dog can be surprisingly agile, quickly coming between them and anyone who might present a threat. In the majority of cases, the Shar Pei will try to pin down an adversary, rather than to bite. On the whole, the Shar Pei is not aggressive but, nonetheless, like other dogs, is perfectly capable of doing damage, and so must be trained to know right from wrong – what the owners will tolerate and what they will not. It is always worth keeping in the back of your mind that the Shar Pei is a good guard. Guarding is instinctive behaviour and, when one considers that the breed was also used as a fighting dog in the past, even though drugs may have been used to excite the fighting instinct, this is a sensible point to remember.

The inventiveness of a Shar Pei can provide many hours of amusement for the onlookers, especially during the stages of growing up. Almost without exception, Shar Pei enjoy games both with other dogs and with humans, and seem to think things out in order to reach decisions about the most appropriate reaction. A sensible owner will help to develop this good judgement.

Carole Lilley with one of her Taiyattang Shar Pei. The unique appearance of the Shar Pei has made it the subject of numerous advertising campaigns.

Photo: Bill Lilley.

Most Shar Pei get on well with children, but it is important that children learn to respect the rights of another living creature.

Photo: Bill Lilley.

All puppies are inquisitive – and this Shar Pei puppy is no exception.

Photo courtesy: Dawne Bullen.

However, one should never allow oneself to forget the Shar Pei's distant ancestors, for instinct is carried down for many generations and must be carefully controlled.

Many Shar Pei seem also to have a hunting instinct, patiently stalking their prey, aided by what is reputed to be exceptional eyesight. It is said that the Shar Pei was also used to hunt boar, in which case, to have been successful against this dangerous animal, the dogs must have had determination, independence and aggression. Some members of the breed seem to enjoy herding, which is often apparent when among younger dogs or small children. Indeed, most Shar Pei seem to adore children, though so much depends on the attitude of the adults as to whether or not the two are taught to intermingle, so that no harm comes to either party.

In most households where more than one Shar Pei is kept, there will be an order of rank among the dogs. Someone will be 'top dog' and as the years go by and the one-time 'top dog' ages, another may take over. This is common to the canine race, but owners should be on their guard, so that no dog suffers damage physically while such changes in leadership are in the throes of taking place.

Shar Pei enjoy playing with each other's faces and legs, gently pulling at them in play. Things which swing also provide great amusement, including tails, whether or not they are attached to another Shar Pei. However, one must be careful to control such games, which can get out of hand if they become too boisterous. As a Shar Pei gets older, it also gets stronger, so rough games

A Shar Pei will fit in with most of the family's activities!   Photo: Bill Lilley.

Shar Pei will usually live alongside other dogs if care is taken during the early stages. Photo courtesy: Wendy Coates.

Taiyattang Uptown Girl is only eight months old, but she is already a powerful animal. She is not standing as she would be expected to in the show ring, but she is showing her lovely head and her horse coat.

Photo: Bill Lilley.

It is important to establish 'house rules' before your Shar Pei gets too big to negotiate with. Taiyattang Chong Hoi Choi is allowed to sleep on this miniature sofa, but if you do not want your dog to go on the furniture you must discipline your puppy at an early stage.

Photo: Bill Lilley.

should be allowed in moderation only. The Shar Pei can mix well with other breeds but, as always, so much depends on the way the different dogs are introduced to each other, and the sensitivity of the owners to any awkward situations which might arise. In some cases the quick reactions of, for example, a Terrier breed, can provoke trouble. With sensible canine management, a Shar Pei can be a most enchanting family member, whether or not other animals share the household.

As an owner of a Shar Pei, you must help the dog to learn what is considered socially acceptable behaviour. Indeed each person has his or her own standards, which vary considerably, and so you will have to let your Shar Pei know what you will tolerate and what you will not. A Shar Pei likes to seek out comfortable spots, so you will have to make it plain which ones are your territory and which ones are the dog's. Always bear in mind that your Shar Pei will grow and, whilst a puppy might fit neatly onto the end of the sofa, considerably more space will be required as that puppy matures – so start as you mean to go on. If you allow something one day and not the next, your Shar Pei, in common with all other canines, will not be able to fathom out the reason why; so be consistent in your commands.

BREED CHARACTERISTICS
The Shar Pei comes in all sorts of colours, some of them in line with the requirements of the Breed Standard, and some of them not. Indeed, it is possible for a single litter to consist of several different colours and even different coat types. Coat lengths vary, the two acceptable types of coat

A six-week-old 'bear-coated' puppy. This type of coat is not acceptable according to the breed standard.

Photo courtesy: Wendy Coates.

The only white Shar Pei known to have been bred in the UK. This puppy has a 'brush-coat'.

Photo: Bill Lilley.

being known as 'horse coat' and 'brush coat', though a longer coat, often referred to as a 'bear coat' also crops up from time to time, though this is not a coat length which is acceptable in terms of the breed standard. One of the breed's authorities in Hong Kong believes that there are, in fact, as many as ten types of coat. It is important to be aware that a horse coat, the shortest of the three principal types, can irritate some sensitive human skin. Often a rash, which appears on a human as a result of the initial introduction, will disappear following repeated contact with the coat, but sometimes it does not. Such a coat feels quite different when stroked in the opposite direction and, when a Shar Pei with this coat is upset, the coat will stiffen still further.

The skin of a Shar Pei is what most people notice first about the breed and, in puppyhood, there is likely to be more abundant wrinkling than in the adult. Because of the wrinkling, attention has to be paid to the skin to be sure that particles of dirt and food do not get trapped and so set up an irritation. The breed also varies to a certain extent in size and, I understand, there is a club in the

USA specialising in 'minis'. However, the normal height range is between eighteen and twenty inches, though in Canada the minimum acceptable height is less, but the Shar Pei is always a dog of some substance. Males are usually somewhat larger than females.

Tails differ considerably from dog to to dog, but they should always be high set. Heads, too, are quite varied – but all the finer points of the breed will be discussed in depth in the chapter concerning analysis of the breed standards. The Shar Pei is a breed which needs careful attention to its eyes, and many breeders tack the eyes of some of their puppies to avoid serious problems. In general, breeders are working hard to eliminate these problems and, certainly, things seem to be moving in the right direction. Without doubt, there are some Shar Pei which encounter no eye problems at all throughout their lives, and dedicated breeders are aiming to make this become the norm.

Shar Pei are an enchanting breed which have captured a great many hearts in their short history in the Western world. They also have a rather endearing habit of face-licking, which seems to extend both to other dogs and to humans. Lastly, do keep in mind that, when asleep, many Shar Pei snore loudly; so, if you are thinking of taking one into your home, you may also need to put aside a little money for some ear muffs!

Chapter Three

THE SHAR PEI IN AMERICA

In 1965 Mr C. M. Chung, who was to become one of the group of people influential in the search for more Shar Pei, bred a Shar Pei puppy, which was exported to the USA the following year. This, it is believed, was the first of the breed to be imported to America. He was named 'Lucky', and was owned by Herman Smith, but was not registered until 1970. Then the Association of American Dog Breeders registered what we now know as the Shar Pei, as the 'Chinese Fighting Dog'. Between 1966 and 1967 five dogs were imported to the USA; three of these had been registered with the Hong Kong and Kowloon Kennel Association. None of these dogs, however, was ever registered with the Chinese Shar Pei Club of America and, unfortunately, there was little interest in the breed in the late 1960s, the breed apparently not having been promoted in any way at all.

A canine magazine in 1971 gave the Shar Pei its first real exposure in the western world, in an article concerning rare breeds. There was a picture of a Shar Pei and a caption stating that this was possibly the last surviving specimen of the breed. There was no reaction to the article, probably because if, as was stated, it was thought to be the last of its kind, those who may have had a potential interest in the survival of the breed expected to face a virtually impossible task.

But things were to change dramatically in 1973, when Hong Kong's Matgo Law put out an appeal in 'Dogs Magazine', in an article entitled "Chinese Fighting Dogs". Matgo Law and Mr Chung were concerned about the fate of the Shar Pei if Hong Kong were to become a part of the People's Republic of China, and it was this which caused them to make such an appeal. "Who knows? If we can ship some dogs to your country, they may some day become as popular as the Pekingese or Chow Chow. We can only hope."

As a direct result of this article, Messrs Law and Chung received numerous enquiries from keen buyers, clearly a demand greater than they could ever have hoped to meet and probably well in excess of what they even dreamed of expecting. This was to mark the real beginning of imports from Hong Kong, Macao and Taiwan, though there were only a few in the years immediately following the appeal.

The new breed brought with it the kind of problems one might have expected, exacerbated by the fact that there was little to work on – other than a Breed Standard which was drawn up by Matgo Law with other knowledgeable breeders in Asia, at the request of owners of the breed in America. It was certainly not possible to trace pedigrees back for several generations, which would, of course, have been of great assistance.

Before analysing the breed standards currently in use and following the progress of the Shar Pei in the USA, I feel it prudent to read carefully the following, the first standard for the Shar Pei in use in America, issued under the auspices of the Hong Kong and Kowloon Kennel Association

LEFT: Am. Ch. Thunder Moon's Bonfire Fury, owned by Pat Gear. America has become an adopted home of the Shar Pei, and there are many important kennels producing top-quality stock.
                    Booth Photography.

BELOW: American bloodlines are often sought-after in the UK and the rest of Europe. These puppies, the result of a mating between Sheng Li Burgundy and CSPCA AKC Ch. Mietung Luv Wun MacMurfee, were born in quarantine in the UK after the bitch was exported in whelp to Linda Rupniak.

Photo courtesy: Linda Rupniak.

(HKKA). It is, however, important to note that this standard was intended as a verbal picture of the ideal Shar Pei, in anticipation of the breed becoming refined when re-established in America. The early Shar Pei in the USA varied greatly both in 'type' and in conformation, and, in actual fact, few of the dogs met the standard as drawn up by the HKKA.

For me, the following Standard gives a very clear picture of how the Shar Pei looked, in the eyes of those people native to the breed's homeland. Having said that, I feel sure that you, like me, will appreciate the reasons why a more generalised Standard, as described in Chapter Five, was necessary. The Standard is reproduced exactly as it was originally written.

PROVISIONAL STANDARD OF CHINESE SHAR PEI
(Hong Kong and Kowloon Kennel Association)

Origin and Characteristics This is a real Chinese breed existing for centuries in the southern provinces near the South China Sea. The original fountain is believed in a town, "Dah Let" in Kwun Tung Province. Dogfighting was the pastime of farmers and small town dwellers since other entertainment was scarcely available then. The breed is equipped with all the features of a gladiator, which will be mentioned by points in the following structural descriptions. The very particular feature is the bluish-black tongue as the Chow Chow. With the addition of the similar dignified expression and excellent guarding instinct, it is believed that both the breeds were from the same origin. However, the Chinese Fighting Dog, as the breed was formerly known, is by no means a smooth-coated Chow. They may come from the same fountainhead or perhaps the former is descended from the latter.

In character, he is not a born fighter, but loves to do so, should the owner provoke since young. Instead, he is a well-balanced dog with a dignified scowling expression; loyal, yet aloof, reserved to strangers while devoted to his family. He needs not be trained; a natural excellent household guard and self-housebroken.

General Appearance An active, compact, short-coupled dog, well knit in frame, giving a square build, standing firm on ground with the calm and firm stature of a severe warrior.

Head and Skull Skull flat and broad, rather large in proportion with the body, with little stop. Profuse and fine wrinkles appear upon the forehead and cheek, and continue to form heavy dewlaps. Muzzle moderately long and broad from the eyes to the point of the nose (without any suggestion of tapering but rather in the mouth-shape of a hippopotamus).

Nose Black, large and wide, occasionally there are cream dogs with brick-colored nose and light fawn dogs with self-colored nose, but black is preferable.

Eyes Dark, small, almond shaped and sunken (light color is found in cream and light fawn dogs). The sunken eyes are advantageous in dog-fighting to reduce chances of injury to the eyes. Also, the sunken eyes and wrinkles upon the forehead help the scowling expression of the breed.

Mouth Teeth strong and level, giving scissor bite, the canines are somewhat curved (increasing the difficulty of freeing the grip). Tongue bluish-black. Flews and roof of mouth black. Gums preferably black.

Ears Small, rather thick, equilateral triangular in shape and slightly rounded at the tip, set well forward over the eyes and wide apart. In contrast to the Chow Chow the ears should set as tightly to the skull and as small as possible. It minimizes the opportunity of the opponent to get a grip on the ears. Some specimens have ears so small as the size of a human thumb nail, just covering the ear burr.

Neck Strong, full, set well on the shoulders with heavy folding skin and abundant dewlaps.

Forequarters Shoulders muscular and sloping. Forelegs straight, of moderate length with good bone.

Body Chest broad and deep, back short; topline, slightly dipped behind the withers, rises to meet the root of the tail, which is set high on the loin. Echoing the wrinkles and dewlaps, there is a lot of skin folding on the body. The abundant loose skin allows spaces for the warrior to turn and attack even though a certain part of the body is gripped by his opponent.

Hindquarters Hindlegs muscular and strong, hocks slightly bent and well let down, giving length and strength from loins to hock. (Not so straight as the Chow.)

Feet Moderate in size, compact and firmly set, toes well split up, with high knuckles giving firm stand.

Tail Thick and round at the base, then evenly tapering to a fine point. The three ways of tail carriage are described as follows, in order of merit: The most desirable is the type set on top and curled over to either side – some curled so tightly as to present the shape of a small ringlet, only in the size of a large ancient China coin. The second type is curled in a loose ring. The third type is carried high in a curve toward the back, not touching the back. This carriage allows the dog to wiggle in a happier and more eager fashion. On either type, the tail should be set high on the loin, showing the anus.

Coat Another peculiar feature of the breed. The coat is extremely short (shorter than the Bulldog's and a similar coat is considered as to be too long) and bristly, unusually harsh to touch. It is a coat absolutely uncomfortable to be held in any canine mouth. It is not lustrous as the coat of a Doberman but by no means gives the impression of an unhealthy coat.

Colour Whole colours – black, red, deep fawn, light fawn and cream, frequently shaded (the underpart of tail and back of thighs of a lighter colour but not in patches or parti-coloured).

Weight and Size Around 18-20 inches at withers; weight 40-50 lbs. Dog is heavier than bitch and more squarely built. The balance of an individual is important.

Faults Spotted tongue. Tail carried horizontally or covering the anus. A flat, long, shining coat (the coat is not harsh and off-standing). Tapering muzzle like a fox (not blunt enough).

VARIATIONS IN TYPE

The early imports to the USA varied widely in type; many displayed major faults and carried genetic problems. People who became involved in the breed in the USA also varied widely, both in their depth of experience in dogs and in their ethics. Thankfully, some dedicated enthusiasts of the Shar Pei were already knowledgeable breeders of other dogs; others were new to dogs but were willing to learn. On the negative side, it was abundantly clear that there was a demand for this new, and unusual, breed and there were those who saw it as an opportunity to make money fast. Those of us who know anything at all about successful breeding realise that, without the utmost care and attention to breeding plans, it is all too easy for things to go wrong; and, as I have said, besides these new imports, the only tool then in the hands of potential Shar Pei breeders was the breed standard quoted above. Reflecting, as it does, the combined knowledge of breeders in Asia, it gives a mental picture of the Shar Pei which was historically correct.

The breeders who were to develop the Shar Pei in the USA did, indeed, carry out much experimentation in the early years but, whilst some followed careful breeding programmes, others did not – their aim seemingly being just to produce a large number of dogs in the shortest possible time. This resulted in a wide variety of specimens of differing type, many of which did not conform to the standard. Indeed, though I suspect it was an exaggeration, it was even said that there was a Shar Pei for each of the seven American Kennel Club Groups, ranging from Toy to Working! With time, and thanks to those genuinely dedicated to the breed, consistency in type began to develop, though there are still variations, as is only to be expected after such disparity in the very early years.

THE START OF THE SHAR PEI CLUB

By 1974 quite a few people had imported stock; certainly enough to decide, rightly, that an organisation had to be formed to help guide the breed along the correct lines and be a means of pooling knowledge and experiences. The first organisational meeting of the Chinese Shar Pei Club of America (CSPCA) was held in Vida, Oregon, on April 26th 1974. Those who attended were Lois E. Alexander, Ernest Albright, John and Nadine Purcell, and Carl Sanders as Acting President.

The earliest imported Shar Pei to be registered with the new CSPCA (CSPCA-6) was bred by Y. K. Leung in Macau on May 28th 1973. This was Down-Homes Kung Fu who had arrived in the USA on July 6th 1973. Imported from Matgo Law by De-Jon and Victor Seas of Ohio, he was the product of a mating between Kay-Fay and Luck-Son, both of which were black. Kung Fu, known as 'Stormy', also a black, had a tropical fungal infection which necessitated his being in quarantine before arriving in his new home.

A photograph of Kung Fu, taken in the kitchen of his owners' American home, serves as a lesson to us all how things can be misconstrued if they fall into unscrupulous hands. The photo was sent out, by the Seas, to those enquiring about the breed. It eventually wended its way to the editor of America's Shar Pei magazine, 'The Barker', described as an example of a native Chinese Fighting Dog pictured in Hong Kong! Fortunately, the error was discovered before publication.

Kung Fu was the first Shar Pei to be shown at a national rare breeds show and, at this, he had the honour of being awarded Best in Show. His early death came on November 22nd 1979, caused by bloat. Fortunately a son of his, Am. Ch. Walnut Lane's China Foo, born in 1975, was still alive at the age of thirteen, when he was the oldest known living Shar Pei in the country.

Ernest and Madeline Albright had been amongst the first to respond to Matgo Law's appeal and their Down-Homes Mui-Chu was another of the earliest imports. A three year old fawn bitch, she arrived on August 20th 1973, having been whelped in Macau and imported, again from Matgo Law. Although she had been mated in Hong Kong prior to export, she did not produce the litter which was hoped for. It was reported in 'The Barker' that Mui-Chu was loaded with heartworms upon arrival in the USA but from these she recovered. Unfortunately, she died of bloat in January of 1976. Mui-Chu was the first Chinese Shar Pei to be shown in America, in December 1973, at the Golden Gate Kennel Club Show.

Soon after Mui-Chu's arrival, an eight week old dog, Down-Homes China Souel, also arrived at the Albrights' Ho Wun kennels. China Souel was born on October 21st 1973 and has been described by his owners as a short-coated fawn, measuring eighteen inches at shoulder and weighing forty-eight pounds. He is reported to have taken many Best in Show awards and reached the age of twelve years. China Souel's litter mate, Down-Homes China Love, also arrived in the USA in late 1973. Owned by the Seas, she was to become the dam of Am. Ch. Walnut Lane's China Foo. Sadly China Love died soon after whelping the litter which produced China Foo.

Lois Alexander, too, had received one of the earliest imports, Down-Homes Little Pea, whelped on November 17th 1971 in Hong Kong. She arrived at San Francisco Airport on October 21st 1973. Three years later, in 1976, Little Pea was to have a less happy experience in that same airport; on her way to a mating (which I gather did not, eventually, take place), she escaped from her kennel and was lost for two and a half days!

THE SHAR PEI CLUB TAKES SHAPE

A second meeting of the new club was held in July 1974. Ernest Albright was elected President and the Albrights' daughter, Darlene Wright, took up the office of Secretary-Treasurer. Walter Skinner became Vice-President and Registrar; Mrs Victor Seas, another early recipient of imported stock, was asked to establish a breed registry. The possibility of future American Kennel Club recognition for the Chinese Shar Pei was discussed. At subsequent meetings, in 1975 and 1976, the same officers were re-elected and, although more breeders attended them, progress regarding registration was still very much in its early stages.

It was the Albrights' Down-Homes China Souel who had the honour of receiving the very first pedigree certificate issued by the new club, and Down-Homes Mui-Chu was the second registration. Matgo Law had exported twenty-one of the first hundred Shar Pei registered, nineteen others were bred by the Albrights, thirteen by Mrs Victor Seas and ten by Walter Skinner. Sixteen different people owned the other thirty-seven Shar Pei registered.

By the next meeting, in February of 1976, it transpired that, although there were thirty known breeders of Chinese Shar Pei, only nineteen of these were members of the club. At this meeting the official name of the breed was decided upon and the breed standard was revised. Minimum prices were also set for the sale of puppies and for stud fees. A minimum stud fee was to be $200 and a minimum price for a puppy, with future potential, was to be $500. Some dogs did, though, sell for higher prices – around $1,000.

STARTING TO SHOW
Until now it had not been easy to find opportunities to show this new breed, though Down-Homes Mui-Chu and China Souel were exhibited on the West Coast. In 1976 Chinese Shar Pei entries were supported for the first time, at The Ohio Rare Breeds Dog Show on April 24th and, later, at the Pacific Coast Hairless Dog Association and Rare Breeds Dog Match on May 30th of the same year. By 1978 there were enough Shar Pei being exhibited to warrant putting on a specialty show. Held at Hinckley, in Illinois, the show was combined with the first annual meeting of the CSPCA. The winner of the coveted title of Best of Breed was Walnut Lane's China Loo, owned by Mrs Victor Seas, with Ernest Albright's Albright's Fawn, going Best Opposite Sex.

However, although a meeting was held in conjunction with the show, a division then occurred between members of the club, and another club was formed. It was not long, however, before the two groups re-united. The Chinese Shar Pei Club of America Inc. was formed and the registrations with each of the two clubs were combined.

FIRST CONFORMATION TITLES
CSPCA Ch. Sis Q's Fu Man Chew, bred by Lois Alexander, owned by California's Jack and Bettye Small, was the first Shar Pei to be awarded an honorary championship. He was born in October 1978, sired by Ellen Weathers Debo's Shir Du Sam Ku out of Down Homes Little Pea. Fu Man Chew, and indeed his sire, were to become the sire of many champions. Fu Man Chew's daughter, Miss Magoo Chew, a daughter of Fu Man Chew, won the first honorary championship title awarded to a bitch. She was born in March 1980, bred by Jack Small and owned by Bettye Small.

RESOLVING PROBLEMS
It is difficult for those of us interested and involved in the Shar Pei, in countries other than America, to absorb the sheer magnitude of the numbers involved. The club grew dramatically during the early 1980s so that, by 1987, there were over five thousand voting members of the Chinese Shar Pei Club of America Inc. and, on average, there were between sixty and one hundred dogs at a show, with several hundred being exhibited at a national specialty. This increase in popularity, though rewarding in many ways, must, surely, have brought with it the inevitable problems which go hand in hand with such a rapid increase in numbers. Nonetheless, the Shar Pei

had truly found its place on the American show-scene – and was there to stay.

Those who were members of the original Chinese Shar Pei Club of America, as I indicated earlier, decided that it would be preferable if a more generalised standard was drawn up. This was done and circulated to the thirty known Shar Pei owners in the USA at that time. Every recipient was invited to either adopt, reject or modify each of the thirty-two statements made in the proposed revised standard, and it was at this point that breeders in Hong Kong and America differed and their ways began to part, each aiming for a different ideal.

One can imagine the confusion which reigned at this difficult time in the breed's formation in the USA. The Chinese Shar Pei Club of America broke up and, as has been said, two separate clubs were formed. Yet another standard, one which made further allowances, got into print. However, by 1982 the two clubs had become reunited, and a revised standard for the Shar Pei was adopted.

THE REVISED STANDARD
References to fighting dogs and to the Chow Chow were deleted; this was the time when the first reference to padding in the muzzle appeared and light purple, spotted or 'flowered' mouths became acceptable.

As the various tail permutations had been prolific, the description of the tail was generalised when it came to drawing up the new standard, stating only that it should curl over the back. A sentence in the new standard which caused confusion and misinterpretation, was: "No tail is a major fault." I must admit to having read this time and time again before realising how it could be misinterpreted, for I had taken it to mean, as was intended, that if a Shar Pei had no tail at all, that was to be considered a major deviation from breed type. However, some, apparently, took it to mean, literally, that whatever the tail was like it would not be considered a major fault, or words to that effect. As a result, several dogs, with little or no tail, continued to be placed highly at shows.

Other generalisations included those concerning coat; instead of requiring a coat which was "extremely short", one which was over one inch in length was considered a major fault. Strangely, there was no reference to the harsh texture of the coat, simply a statement that it should appear healthy, "without being shiny or lustrous". No colour specification was made, other than that it was to be a whole colour.

Height remained as specified previously, but the weight range was increased by five pounds in each direction, thus allowing for a heavier and more muscular dog to fall within the standard. Personally, though, I find it difficult to imagine a typical Shar Pei weighing as little as thirty-five pounds. A very positive inclusion in the revised standard was the clause describing correct gait for the Shar Pei.

This new standard came into effect in October 1982 and remained in force until yet another revised standard was issued in 1985 – with still more revisions appearing later. As so many Shar Pei breed standards have been in use, in such a short space of time, I feel it could confuse readers to include each in its entirety. Instead you will find the current American and English standards in the next chapter and, I hope, you will, from time to time, refer back to the original HKKA standard for the sake of reference – and its visual memory.

AMERICAN KENNEL CLUB ACCEPTANCE
May 8th 1988 was a landmark in the history of the Shar Pei in America, for that was the day on which the American Kennel Club accepted the breed in its Miscellaneous category. In August 1992 the Chinese Shar Pei Club was accepted into the AKC. Its first show, after acceptance by the AKC, was held at the Westminster All Breed Show in Madison Square Garden, New York, in 1993. At this show, limited to Champions, Shar Pei drew the second largest entry.

Am. Ch. Thunder Moon's Chicago Fire (pictured at 17 months): The first AKC Champion Shar Pei, owned and bred by Colleen Kehe.

Photo courtesy: Colleen Kehe.

MAJOR INFLUENCES

I have already mentioned the sheer magnitude of the numbers of Shar Pei registrations. This, alone, would make it an impossible task to do justice to the many people who have played an important role in the breed's development over the years. For example, at a breed show, numbers can be in the region of 500 dogs entered, with with the 1994 National Specialty bringing in a total entry of over 800. In past years there has been as many as 1,200 entries. Such enormous figures have meant that there can be as many as sixty Shar Pei exhibited in one class – many times in excess of the sorts of numbers one could expect at a similar show in Europe. Voting membership of the breed club runs into several thousand people, many of whom exhibit several Shar Pei. This necessitates full-time staff, as well as numerous volunteers, to assist in managing this thriving club.

Added to the sheer numbers of Shar Pei in the USA, it is also necessary to consider the great size of that country and to remember that a situation found in one area may not be the same elsewhere. All-breed shows vary across the United States, for example, in the Pacific Northwest, entries vary from between twenty to over seventy.

THE FIRST AKC CHAMPION

Am. Ch. Thunder Moon's Chicago Fire, who had gained his CSPCA championship title in May 1991, at the age of seven and a half months, became the very first AKC Champion Shar Pei, on August 9th, 1992. Owned by Colleen Kehe, who lives in Illinois and has bred and shown Shar Pei for over twelve years, 'Matches' was out of Am. Ch. Thunder Moon's Happy Feet MT., so named because she had an engaging habit of hitting Colleen with her paw whenever she wanted attention. In turn, Matches has perfected this pawing trait and it has also become apparent in some of his offspring.

The show career of Am. Ch. Thunder Moon's Chicago Fire is an enviable one, especially for one

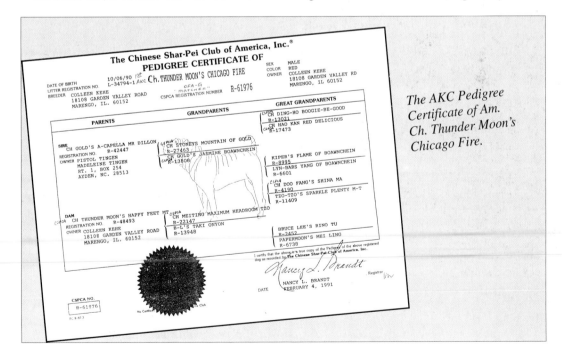

The AKC Pedigree Certificate of Am. Ch. Thunder Moon's Chicago Fire.

Am. Ch. Thunder Moon's Firehouse Rag (left) and Am. Ch. Thunder Moon's Miss Le Toe, both Champion offspring of Am. Ch. Thunder Moon's Chicago Fire.

Photo: Colleen Kehe.

so young. A multiple Best in Breed Specialty winner, it only took three 5-Point Majors from the puppy classes for him to complete his CSPCA title. The most memorable win for his owner was first at the CSPCA National Specialty Show's Stud Dog class in Irvine, at which time he was still only nineteen months old. When he gained his AKC championship title, the first for a Shar Pei, there were then ninety thousand registered Shar Pei. His AKC title was completed quickly, with three 5-Point Majors on August 7th, 8th and 9th, at the Ballston Spa Cluster, New York. He also became eligible for his ROM, for eleven of his offspring completed their championship titles within the space of a year. One of Matches' successful offspring, Am. Can. Ch. Flying Colours Strike a Match, produced Best of Winners at the National, a year after the same achievement by Matches.

Colleen Kehe has very kindly made available some of her own perceptions about the breed and it is, I believe, interesting to listen to her views, as she has been so involved with the Shar Pei in America. She feels it is always easier to develop a head or wrinkle than it is to improve on fronts or structure and she, personally, stays towards what she considers "the moderate in type". She would also like to see more horse-coats in the ring, for she believes it is possible to have both substance and type with such a coat, though many horse-coated specimens appear to lack reach and drive. Sharen Jud is apparently someone who has bred some very good horse-coats.

Another area to which Colleen feels breeders need to turn their attention is using dogs with good bites in their breeding programmes, in an endeavour to reproduce this characteristic. In her opinion, there should not be the number of bad bites which are regrettably found and, seemingly, accepted by some breeders. Whilst fronts still need to be worked on, they have already improved greatly and, she considers, the breed should ideally be more uniform in size and in bone.

Of course there have been many Shar Pei who have had an impact on the breed in the USA. In Colleen Kehe's opinion Am. Ch. Gold's A-Capella Mr Dillon is a true ambassador, as is Am. Ch. Meiting Luv Wun MacMurfee who has done a great deal for the breed by producing good dogs which have been consistent in type, while CSPCA Ch. Stoney's Mountain of Gold also had influence but was not used at stud in the USA for very long. She sees Am. Ch. Alpha Autumn Glo Nordic Star, owned by Cathy Little, as having the potential to become a top brood bitch, and Am. Ch. Down-Homes Happy Ambassador was one of her favourites. Amongst other Shar Pei which Colleen holds in high regard are CSPCA Ch. Yu Mi-Te-Man Tzo Tzo, CSPCA Ch. Shir Du Bang, CSPCA Ch. Shangrila Gogrila T'baggy and Am. Ch. Chesapeake's Beamme Up Scotty.

KATHY KAMAKEEAINA
Kathy Kamakeeaina had been involved in Samoyeds for many years and, also, a breeder of Maltese, when the Shar Pei moved into her life 1987, when she bought a bitch who produced Am. Ch. Maka Jaba the Hutt, who finished his CSPCA title at eleven months of age. The Hutt was the Number 1 horse coat Shar Pei in the USA, with nine Specialty Bests in one year, from September to December of 1990. In Southern California he was the first Shar Pei to be placed in the Non-Sporting Group. CSPCA Ch. Lotsalips Maka Lea produced Best of Breed winner Am. Ch. Maka Cindel of Weenklebomb, whilst the Hutt, mated to Lotsalips, produced Am. Ch. Maka Sy Snoodle, who won a Best in Show Rare Breeds award as well as becoming the sixth top Shar Pei in the nation in 1993. The latest champion sired by the Hutt is Am. Ch. Maka Jaba Jabar who finished his title all from the 'Bred By' class.

In Kathy Kamakeeaina's opinion, the Shar Pei has come along way towards being accepted by the AKC, and the breed, now, has better temperaments than ever before. She feels, too that the skin is much improved, as is general soundness.

OTHER INFLUENCES
Many people have worked hard in the USA to continue to improve the breed and give advice to others. For twelve years **Betsy Davison,** of the Loong Ch'ai Kennel, was the CSPCA's representative to the Orthopedic Foundation for Animals (OFA), and author of a book about the Shar Pei puppy.

Mary Ellen Tarman, based in Pennsylvania, has been involved with Shar Pei since 1983 and, in August 1993, took over as breed historian. In that month she also put together a comprehensive review of available books about the Shar Pei, which I feel sure was of tremendous help to the Shar Pei fraternity throughout the world. This was published in Purebred Dogs/American Kennel Gazette.

Jo Ann Redditt, also involved in the breed, is a writer, artist and editor, and there must, surely,

Am. Ch. Chesapeake's Sizzler: This deep mahogany red male is pictured winning a Best Opposite Sex award.
                    Photo: Booth Photography.

CSPCA AKC Ch. Maka Cindel of Weenklebomb.

        Photo courtesy: Kathy Kamakeeaina.

CSPCA AKC Ch. Maka Jaba the Hutt: Winner of nine Specialties in one year. Owned by Kathy Kamakeeaina.

Photo courtesy: Kathy Kamakeeaina.

Lindsey's Christian Dior showing promise as a youngster.

Photo courtesy: Bill and Carole Lilley.

be countless people in the Shar Pei world who are much indebted to her for her skill in this field. Jo Ann and Duncan Redditt introduced Down-Homes Prophet as their first Shar Pei in their Go-Lo kennels, having previously been involved with Lhasa Apsos. Down-Homes Fortune Cookie joined soon after and, from her first litter, one of the puppies earned a Companion Dog title in the Obedience ring. Jo Ann helped to organise the Mid-Atlantic Chinese Shar Pei Club.

Maryann Smithers has also competed in the Obedience ring with dogs from her Oriental Treasure kennels. Bedlam's Panda was her first Shar Pei to get her championship title and, also, the first to gain her Companion Dog title.

Cathi Schneider has been involved with the breed for a long while and is President of the Chinese Shar Pei Club of America. She is also the club's representative to the American Kennel Club.

Michael Litz and Pamela Hurley, of Alpha Reg Kennel, had their foundation bitch, Hurley's Shen Te Mi, from **Ellen Weathers Debo** in California, herself an author of a most informative book about the breed.

Lindsey's Yin Chelsea Yoko at Taiyattang, pictured in the USA at eighteen months of age, prior to being exported to the Lilleys in the UK.

Photo courtesy: Bill and Carole Lilley.

Shirley and Larry Rafferty acquired their first Shar Pei in 1977 and started their Dor Mon kennel the following year. The words 'Dor Mon' mean 'lots of wrinkles' in Chinese. This was the year in which they contacted Matgo Law in Hong Kong, and they bought two bitches and a dog, Down-Homes Unicorn, who was eventually exported to the UK. The Laffertys later imported Down-Homes Black Woo Loos, who became a CSPCA double Champion, winning conformation and Obedience titles. CSPCA Ch. Dor Mon's Tao Tzu (alled peached) lived to the age of ten , producing six Champions in her three litters, which gave her a Register of Merit with the CSPCA.

One of Peaches' offspring, Ch. Dor Mon's Li Te, produced AKC Ch. Dor Mon's Chin Ho, who, in 1993, was the first Chinese Shar Pei to win Best of Breed at Westminster Kennel Club Show. That year 'Chin' finished number 8 Shar Pei in the US in Breed and All Breed standings, and was placed fourth in Canada.

Jo Ann Webster also had her first introduction to Shar Pei through Ellen Weathers Debo in 1977, when she was anxious to see the rare dog which Ellen had imported from Hong Kong. An interesting comment some years ago from Jo Ann Webster is that she believes the brush coats have a stronger immune system and that, when crossed with short-coated dogs, the puppies have both better health and better temperament.

It is fascinating to hear how different people learned about the Shar Pei in the early years. A picture of two puppies in 'National Geographic World' was originally responsible for the setting up of **Dick and Zell Llewellyn's** Shoestring Acres, while **June Collins** first saw a Shar Pei photograph in a Vancouver newspaper in 1970. Seven years later she found an advert in the *Los Angeles Times* for a 'Chinese Fighting Dog', which eventually led to the formation of the Three

Am. Ch. Dor Mon's Trail Blazer, owned by Shirley Rafferty.

Photo: Steven Ross.

Am. Ch. Dor Mon's Chin Ho: Best of Breed at Westminster 1993, owned by Shirley Rafferty.

Photo: Chuck and Sandy Tatham.

Sisters kennel. Pictures in a children's magazine first sparked the interest of **Bob and Dawn Walling**, owners of Boawnchien Kennel. **Shirley and Doug Skinner** obtained their original stock from Ohio and also imported from Hong Kong; they feel that they have been able to increase muzzle size and produce a more square build in the dogs produced in their Shir Du kennel. The Bruce Lee kennel, operated by **Bruce Lee Resnick,** has produced much stock of note and has helped to promote the breed by having Shar Pei appear in magazine articles and advertisements. **Pat Gear** of the Mi-Kumar kennel has been involved with Shar Pei for seven years. One of her own Champions, Am. Ch. Thunder Moon's Bonfire Fury has won nine Best of Breed, eleven Best Opposite Sex, and a Group 2 win at only two and a half years of age.

CSPCA Ch. Down-Homes Black Woo Loo CD.

Photo courtesy: Shirley Rafferty.

FIRST COMPANION AND OBEDIENCE TITLES IN THE USA

June 7th, 1981 was the date on which Tian Shan's Mikee was awarded his obedience title. He was bred by Bettye Small and owned by Murray and Bonnie Miller.

Rosie Lucitt is the owner and trainer of Fritt's Han-Ho-Yan CDX who had his Companion Dog Excellent title awarded in December 1982, the first Shar Pei dog to receive this award. At the time of his death in September 1984 he was working on his utility degree. Rosie Lucitt also bred, owned and trained the first Shar Pei bitch to earn the CDX degree, Danros-U-Weoof-O, Am. CD, Hon. CDX TDI. This bitch's sire was Han-Ho-Yan; her dam also received her Companion Dog title. What a wonderful combination of breeding and training!

After the Shar Pei was recognised, the first dog to obtain the AKC Companion Dog title was Joan Edeen's Am. Ch. Sui Yeen's Marco Polo.

The Shar Pei has clearly had a great impact on the canine world in America and there is no doubt that American bloodlines can now be found throughout the world. Only yesterday, at a UK show, I found myself looking at recent photographs of a Shar Pei litter with an American sire and dam. The bitch was exported to the UK in whelp and so the puppies were born in quarantine. The world seems to get smaller almost by the minute and, as it does so, the strength of the Shar Pei increases.

Chapter Four

THE SHAR PEI WORLDWIDE

UNITED KINGDOM

THE FIRST IMPORT

As Britain moved into the 1980s, a new breed of dog was about to hit the headlines. Good Friday of 1981 was the actual day on which the first Shar Pei, Heathstyle Dandelion, arrived on Britain's shores. A fawn dog, with a horse coat, he was bred in the USA by Ruth Fink and imported by Heather Ligget. 'Dan', as he was known, was a great ambassador for the breed, appearing on many television shows and, more importantly, siring some top winning stock, including Danish, Lux. Ger. Ch. Heathstyle Dragonwort, Heathstyle Edelweis of Delkris, Heathstyle Marshmallow, Fearghas Hak Fu, Burgoynes Oriental Charmer and Burgoynes China Tea, to name but a few offspring of note. His bloodlines live on in the generations which have followed and it is interesting to note that, in maturity, Dan weighed sixty pounds and was twenty inches in height.

Being the very first import to the UK, his pedigree will be of interest to many:-

```
                                    Down-Homes King Kong
                     Down-Homes Prophet
                                    Down-Homes Fleur
         Cooks Ping Pong
                                    Down-Homes  Jim Jade
                     Down-Homes  Suzy Que
                                    Down-Homes Don Kar


   Heathstyle Dandelion


                                    Down-Homes  Man Poon
                     Rogeans Loy of Wyloway
                                    Albright's Loo Mang
         Rogeans Snookums of Wyloway
                                    Walnut Lanes China Foo
                     Walnut Lanes Shao Nu
                                    Shir-Du No Li
```

LEFT: Heathstyle Dandelion, pictured as a youngster. The first Shar Pei to reach Britain. He was imported from the USA by Heather Ligget.

BELOW: Heathstyle Dandelion became a great ambassador for the breed and sired winning stock in the show ring.

Both photographs courtesy: Dulcie Ligget.

THE FIRST BITCH

Later on in 1981 Heather Ligget also imported a bitch, from Matgo Law in Hong Kong. She was Down-Homes Junoesque of Heathstyle, the only bitch to have been imported directly from Hong Kong and registered by the English Kennel Club. Known as 'Honeysuckle', she had a red brush coat, weighed about fifty pounds and measured approximately nineteen inches in height. Again, her pedigree will be of interest as, mated to Dandelion, she was to produce the UK's first litter of Shar Pei puppies:-

```
                                        Down-Homes King Kong
                         Down-Homes Prince of Darkness
                                        Down-Homes Fleur
                  Down-Homes Royal Zeal
                                        Down-Homes Un Long
                         Dragon Lady's Jasmine of Gun Club
                                        Dragon Lady
```

Down-Homes Junoesque of Heathstyle

```
                                        Down-Homes Bobby
                         Down-Homes Ji Jade
                                        Down-Homes Don Lin
                  Down-Homes Black Bonnie
                                        Down-Homes Prince of Darkness
                         Down-Homes Black Wong Ding
                                        Down-Homes Oriental Star
```

Down-Homes Junoesque of Heathstyle, bred by Matgo Law. The only Shar Pei imported from Hong Kong to be registered by the English Kennel Club.

Photo courtesy: Dulcie Ligget.

Down-Homes Junoeque of Heathstyle with her first litter of puppies. This was the first Shar Pei litter born in the UK, bred by Heather Ligget. The sire was Heathstyle Dandelion.

Photo courtesy: Dulcie Ligget.

INFLUENTIAL IMPORTS

Interest had been kindled and enthusiasm fired. The following year brought with it more new imports. Bred by Eve Olsen of the famous Willowledge Kennels, Burgoynes Suzy May Wong and Burgoynes Snow Dragon were brought into the country by Pat Pearce, to be joined by Highlight of Hong Kong and Blossom of Hong Kong from Richard Beauchamp's Hong Kong kennels in the USA. Burgoynes Snow Dragon, a fawn brush-coated bitch, proved to be one of the most influential imports in Pat Parke's breeding programme, and puppies produced in her litters have gone on to form the foundation stock of many well-known kennels. Many influential dogs were produced from her, including Burgoynes Tai Piao Te, who was exported to Germany after a short, but successful, show career in the UK.

Highlight of Hong Kong at Burgoyne was affectionately known as 'Big Buddha', a sixty-pound dog, standing twenty inches at shoulder, with a cream brush coat. He was one of the last sons of Down-Homes Clown Nosed Buddha, legendary as one of the true Chinese fighting dogs, who had been left for dead after a dog-fight – until Matgo Law noticed a slight movement and took him home to nurse him back to health. Clown Nosed Buddha went on to become one of the most important Shar Pei stud dogs in the breed's history. Big Buddha was anxious to please and became an important stud dog as he was also willing to please the ladies, however unresponsive they may have been! He sired several notable progeny but, sadly, died unexpectedly of a heart attack in December of 1987.

Heather Ligget added Heathstyle Tumbleweed, Willowedge Ah Fuk and Tshimaos Deng Ho to her own kennel, whilst Raymond Boatwright imported Willowedge Emanuelle and Willowedge Casanova. In addition to these, Heather Sweeting, now Honorary Secretary of the Shar Pei Club of Great Britain, brought Willowedge Razzamataz and ZL's Black Opal into the the country, whilst Tshimaos Deng joined Nigel Marsh and Terry Purse.

Heather Sweeting's Willowedge Razzamataz was bred by Eve Olsen-Fisher, in January 1982. A red fawn, horse-coated bitch, she measured nineteen inches and weighed forty-five pounds in maturity. Though rarely shown, she had a delightful, gentle and loving temperament and produced three litters which included some notable offspring. She died just one week before reaching the

Heathstyle Tumbleweed, pictured as a puppy while still in quarantine. Tumbleweed was imported from the USA in 1982.

Photo courtesy: Dulcie Ligget.

age of eight. Heather Sweeting's US import, ZL's Black Opal of Fearghas, came to the UK in August 1982, having been bred in Dick and Zella Llewellyn's Shoestring Acres kennel in Texas. Again, I include her pedigree, for it can be traced back to some of the original Chinese stock which was sent to the USA. Her grandsire, Tai Li of Tai Lu, owned by William Morrison, was born in China and her grand-dam, Shouson, born also in 1977, came from Robert Chan's kennels in Hong Kong. ZL's Black Opal was known as 'Chippy', because she apparently looked like a chocolate chip cookie in colour, when her new owner had really been expecting a black. She was sixteen and a half inches tall, and weighed forty-four pounds, with a horse coat.

	Albright's Ho Hsiung
Shir Du Sam Ku	
	Walnut Lanes China Chen Chu
Hon. Ch. Gold's Rising Sun	
	Gong Bo Ding of Rshaf
Fond of Lao Te	
	Tzo-Tzo's Lu Sing

ZL's Black Opal of Fearghas

	Unknown
Tai Li of Tai Lu	
	Unknown
OB Ch. ZL's Cinnamon Cricket	
	Ah Ha
Shouson	
	Wong Choi

Heathstyle Dandelion and Down-Homes Junoesque were mated and, as I have already mentioned, produced the first litter of Shar Pei puppies to be whelped in the UK, on 29th September 1982. There were five dog puppies in the litter, one of which, Heathstyle Edelweis, achieved success in Britain's show rings in the ownership of Chris and Derek Garratt, who added the suffix Delkris to his name. Known as 'Kendo', he was to become the most successfully campaigned Shar Pei in the UK during the years of 1983, 1984 and 1985. Kendo took Best in Show at the Shar Pei Club's Open Show in 1988, having won the Veteran class, ending an illustrious show career. He had a reputation for being throughly relaxed in the show-ring and always showed himself to perfection. At home, too, he was quiet and easy-going but had no interest in stud work, siring only one litter shortly before his death in 1990. Another from that same litter, Heathstyle Dragonwort, went on to gain championship titles in Germany, Luxembourg and Denmark in the ownership of Germany's Linda Reinhelt.

The year of 1982 was progressing well for the Shar Pei and, in October, only a month after the first litter had been whelped, Burgoynes Snow Dragon produced a litter of nine whelps for owner Pat Pearce. The first UK litter had consisted only of dogs. This one produced the country's first bitches, for there were four in the litter. There was a great deal of publicity surrounding the birth of such unusual-looking puppies, bringing coverage both in the press and on television.

The following year Pat Pearce imported three more Shar Pei, Rosie of Hong Kong, Battle Chief of Hong Kong and Down-Homes US Girl. 'Chief' was whelped in the USA on January 1st 1983 by breeder Richard Beauchamp. He arrived in the UK in December of that year, actually on loan. His show career had already begun in the USA, where he won not only Best Puppy but, also, Reserve Best of Breed at the Chinese Shar Pei Club of America's specialty show in Texas. Whilst still in America he had produced three litters of puppies, but was infertile for a while following his release from quarantine in the UK. As a result, he stayed in the UK longer than had originally been planned, but did sire several litters before his return to the USA in 1987. He is the great grandsire of Burgoynes Pot Black, the first Shar Pei to gain a Junior Warrant and top Shar Pei puppy in 1989. Battle Chief of Hong-Kong's height was twenty-one inches, his weight sixty-five pounds, and his horse coat was fawn in colour.

Down-Homes US Girl was one out of a litter of seven, bred by Matgo Law in Hong Kong. Three of this litter subsequently came to England, from America, where they had been registered with the Chinese Shar Pei Club of America and were, therefore, eligible for registration with the English Kennel Club.

The three from this litter were two bitches, US Girl and Down-Homes Ursula, imported by Lynn Ayles and Gill Wolsey, and a dog, Down-Homes the Unicorn, brought in by Heather Ligget. Miss Liggett also brought in two of June Collins' breeding, Three Sisters Gou Dah, a bitch, and Three Sisters Grey Ling, a dog, as well as Dor-Mons Mary Beth, bred by the Raffertys. Three Sisters Gau Dah of Heathstyle had been whelped in California by breeder June Collins on December 1st 1982 and arrived in the UK early the following year.

Again, he was a fawn with a horse coat, but measured twenty-two inches at shoulder, weighing between fifty-five and sixty pounds. Whilst in the UK he sired several litters and, in all but one of these, there were parti-coloured puppies present. In 1985 'Gou' returned to the USA, to live a life of luxury in a pet home in California.

In view of the fact that it is known and recognised that Three Sisters Gau Dah of Heathstyle produced parti-colours, this is another pedigree of particular interest to dedicated breeders:-

Down-Homes Clown-Nosed Buddha
Down-Homes Union Jack
Down-Homes Fleur
Three Sisters Ah Dah
Down-Homes Ginger Nuts
Yuk Lan
Down-Homes Frumpy

Three Sisters Gau Dah of Heathstyle

Down-Homes Un Long
Dragon Lady's Jess of Gun Club
Dragon Lady
Ming Jue of Three Sisters
Down-Homes Bobby
Down-Homes Frumpy
Down-Homes Lady Charcoal

Also in 1983, Tigereye of Hong Kong was imported, by Pat Pearce, for Ann Davies. From Richard Beauchamp's kennels in the USA, Tigereye, known as 'Tigi', was a black bitch, born on February 2nd 1981. She was to be the foundation bitch of Ann Davies' Sharming kennel and was a daughter of Down-Homes Black Pearl, considered to be one of the best black bitches in the world. Before her death, at the age of seven in 1988, Tigi had produced two litters with four puppies in each. The years were moving ahead and the imported stock slowly increasing, with extremely high prices being paid for some of it. Many of these imports were closely related to one another and, therefore, different dogs made an impact on the breed in different ways; it is therefore difficult to say which had the greatest influence.

1984 heralded a number of imports from Germany. Shar Pei breeder Linda Reinelt sent over Tsihmaos Ging Gong, Tsihmaos Ginger and Tsihmaos Je Go, and later came Kung-Fu's Ek-La-Nit and Samurais A'Feng Zeng of Tsihmaos. Tsihmao's Je-Go of Fearghas, a red brush-coated bitch, was imported by Heather Sweeting at the request of daughter Emma, late in 1984. Not a lover of the show-ring, 'Polly', as this bitch was known, did have two litters of puppies before her untimely death, due to kidney failure, in February 1989, at the age of four and a half. The sire, on both occasions, was Fearghas Hak Fu and several of these outstanding puppies were exported. Three from the first litter went to Australia, one of which, Fearghas Princess Chao Chun, became a Champion, the first foreign champion to have been bred in the UK. Her sister, Fearghas Queen Wa, also gained her title, prior to which she had whelped a litter which produced Australia's first home-bred champion. Another from Polly's first litter went to South Africa.

From Denmark, to Glenda Parkes in the UK, came the fawn, brush-coated China House Danish Explorer at Vanden, the only pure Chinese Diamond-bred Shar Pei in England and only one of a handful of dogs, throughout the world, which has descended from this important kennel in Hong

Kong. As can be seen from the following pedigree, his sire gained titles in Denmark, Luxembourg, Germany and France and it is useful to see how closely he is bred, being the offspring of a full brother to full sister mating, and both sire and dam themselves being the results of father/daughter matings:-

Unknown
Chinese Diamond Ah Choi
Unknown
Dk., Lux., Ger., Fr. Ch. Chinese Diamond Tai Shan
Chinese Diamond Ah Choi
Chinese Diamond Tin Mei
Chinese Diamond Chi Fong

China House Danish Explorer at Vanden

Unknown
Chinese Diamond Ah Choi
Unknown
Chinese Diamond Lai Fung
Chinese Diamond Ah Choi
Chinese Diamond Tin Mei
Chinese Diamond Chi Fong

Heathstyle T. Bear of Chew: Imported from the USA in January 1984.

Photo courtesy: Dulcie Ligget.

Born in September 1984 'Monty', as Danish Explorer is known, was shown lightly as a youngster but made a comeback in the Veteran class of the breed club show in 1992, when he was reputed to have gone around the ring like a two-year-old, to much applause. Used selectively at stud, his litters have produced a high proportion of quality stock which have formed the foundation of many well-known kennels, so his name appears in the pedigrees of much successful stock. At home, where Monty struck up an inseparable friendship with the Parkes' Rottweiler, every Shar Pei in the Vanden kennel is one of Monty's descendants.

Heathstyle T-Bear of Chew was a dog with an interesting pedigree, as his grandsire was Sis-Q's Fu Man Chew, the very first Shar Pei in the USA to be awarded the title of Honorary Champion. Others in the pedigree were also well-known winners in the USA. T-Bear was imported to the UK by Heather Ligget and did sire a few litters but, although a very strong and well-boned dog, unfortunately he had a bobtail, as did the majority of pups which he sired. For a number of reasons his pedigree is, therefore, worthy of inclusion:-

		Ch. Sis-Q's Fu Man Chew
	Adam Fu Chew	
		Madam Seng
Chew's Carbon of Ku		
		Shir Du Ling Fu
	Yu Ha Chew	
		Walnut Lanes China Sea

Heathstyle T-Bear of Chew

		Gong Bo Ding of Eshaf
	Yu Mi-Te Man of Tzo-Tzo	
		Yu Hu
Mite Big Girl of Kuku		
		Ah-Chu of Val-Yet
	Blossom Eng of Val Yet	
		Pong of Val-Yet

Dulcie E Ligget, Hon. Treasurer of the Shar Pei Club of GB, is a breeder of Shar Pei in her own right, holding the Dulfran affix with lines founded on the American and Hong Kong imports, Heathstyle Dandelion and Down-Homes Junoesque of Heathstyle. Amongst Mrs Ligget's winning dogs is Heathstyle Edelweiss of Delkris, for many years the top winning British dog.

Jennie and Steve Baker brought in Tsimao's Fang Yin of Jentiki, at the age of eighteen months; she was the second of their imports. She whelped a litter in August 1985 and one of the puppies, Jentiki Burnt Toast, was exported to Italy, where she became one of the foundation bitches for Isabella Pizzamiglio's Khambaliq kennel. Another, Jentiki Apricot Surprise, became the first winner of the Shar Pei Club's Points Competition in 1986. Jentiki Red Fire Dragon, from a subsequent litter, went to live in Australia.

Still dogs were coming in from the USA and Frank Farrar and Don Wiedon of Wisconsin, who wanted to live in the UK, brought over, amongst others, a bitch in whelp from their Sedeki kennel. Unfortunately, things did not work out as planned, so the gentlemen returned to the USA, taking with them some of the puppies born here and all but one of the adults they had brought with them. However, of those they left, Sedeki Fab-u-Lus Beh won well in the ring and Sedeki Fab-u-Lus Fub-by produced a litter, the sire of which was Sedeki Charee Chan, the only adult male which had not returned to the USA with the owners.

CURRENT BREEDERS

BILL AND CAROLE LILLEY: TAIYATTANGS
Bill and Carole Lilley had bred their first litter while living in London. Two of the offspring went to America and the only dog in the litter became their Ir. Ch. Taiyattangs Smiffy the Last Emperor. In 1989, having made contact with Ellen Weathers Debo, author of 'The Chinese Shar Pei', they found themselves in the USA, spending three weeks searching around many different kennels. They discovered Mel and Marsha Lindsey, of the Lindsey kennels in Florida, whose stock was the result of several years of line breeding. The Lilleys purchased three bitches, all at the same time, and all were mated by different dogs from the Lindsey kennels and sent over to the UK in whelp.

Lindsey's Seductive Scrappy at Taiyattang was one of these. In 1989 she was the first of the three to arrive and she produced two puppies in quarantine – Taiyattangs Shar Long and Taiyattangs Ice on Fire, the first Shar Pei to receive a Best Puppy in Show award when breed classes were on offer at the show. From a later litter of hers, Taiyattangs Chickweed and Taiyattangs Silk Stockings both won Best Puppy awards on their first outing, and Silk Stockings has gone on to become the top winning Shar Pei in England of all time. Scrappy is incredibly gentle with both animals and children and, as such, is a great favourite in the household, especially

Carole Lilley with members of her Shar Pei family.

Photo: Bill Lilley.

Irish Ch. Taiyattangs Smiffy The Last Emperor, pictured at five months.

Photo: Bill Lilley.

Irish Ch. Taiyattangs Silk Stockings: Top winning Shar Pei in the UK.

Photo: Bill Lilley.

with Carole. But it is Silk Stockings' sire, Ir. Ch. Taiyattangs Smiffy the Last Emperor, who is Bill Lilley's favourite. Smiffy has shared top honours with his daughter for three years and, between them, they have taken a significant proportion of top slots at shows throughout the UK and Southern Ireland.

One of the Lilleys' puppies was used in a mammoth advertising campaign for Prudential and so the Shar Pei has again come to the notice of the public in newspapers and bill-boards throughout the country. With all due respect, I have to smile as I recall that the first time I saw this advert: it was lining the floor of one of my own kennels, perhaps not the most public place to be, but it reached an appreciative audience!

Sami was the next to arrive but, unfortunately, she did not produce the litter which had been hoped for, though she did have a litter soon after; Chelsea produced four puppies in quarantine, the most notable of which was Taiyattangs Gracelands, top puppy in the breed in 1991.

Burgoynes Imagination at Konishiki (pictured at five months): The top Shar Pei bitch in 1989, and the first to obtain a KC Junior Warrant.

Photo courtesy: Linda Rupniak.

LINDA AND LUKE RUPNIAK: KONISHIKI

Linda and Luke Rupniak formed their Konishiki kennel some seven years ago, Linda having fallen for the Shar Pei whilst showing her Dobermann. Her first Shar Pei, Burgoynes Imagination at Konishiki, known as 'Ginny', was Top Shar Pei Bitch in 1989 and the first to obtain the Kennel Club's Junior Warrant. A red fawn horse coat, Ginny has not only won well in the ring herself, but has also produced some notable offspring. From her first litter, to Yacanto Fruitcake, Linda's second Shar Pei, there were two Junior Warrant winners, Konishiki Special Brew and Konishiki Fatal Attraction; both are males and each has sired promising litters. Fatal Attraction's daughter, Isolas Grand Marnier, has followed in the footsteps of her father and grand-dam, winning a Junior Warrant; added to which she has won green stars in Ireland. In Ginny's second litter to the same stud, there was also a Warrant winner; and a chocolate-coloured bitch, which unfortunately did not survive beyond ten weeks, due to a respiratory complaint. Linda is honest enough to comment on the fact that Ginny's third litter, to an outside stud, did not produce typey Shar Pei. However, her fourth litter, to Jordansville Baby Boxcar at Peandokry, with an American sire and dam, produced what her breeder considers her best litter. She feels that Boxcar helped to make the ears small and tighten tails, and yet retained good fronts.

Yacanto Fruitcake, a dilute known as 'Khan', though a sound dog, had ears on the large side and, despite a good start in the ring, unfortunately suffered from demodetic mange, which was cured with herbal remedies in the space of eight months. Linda Rupniak decided to retire Khan from stud as he suffered a few bouts of Shar Pei Hock Syndrome, something which she has researched personally and has found to be hereditary.

Yoshia Hooray Hallelujah, 'Maddy' to her friends, the third Shar Pei to join the Konishiki kennel, has thankfully been blessed with no problems at all and has enjoyed a spectacular show career, becoming Top Shar Pei Puppy for 1991 and winning a Junior Warrant. She took Best of

*Yoshia Hooray
Hallelujah at
Konishiki: Top Shar
Pei Puppy 1991,
Best of Breed, Crufts
1992.*

*Photo courtesy:
Linda Rupniak.*

*Am. Ch. Sheng Li
Mon Ju Copious
(Am. Ch. Sag's Mtn.
High Red Express –
Am. Ch. Dor Mon's
Mal Lite) imported
from the USA in
1994.*

*Photo: Carol Ann
Johnson.*

Breed at Cruft's in 1992, when she was just over a year old. In her only litter to date she produced six puppies, one of which is Konishiki Willow the Wisp, retained by the Rupniaks, and which achieved Top Puppy Shar Pei for 1993 – particularly rewarding with a home-bred bitch.

Luke and Linda Rupniak have been realistic about the problems they have encountered and aim to improve the breed, using Maddy and Willow in future breeding programmes. They are particularly concerned about Shar Pei Hock Syndrome and intend to campaign to eradicate this by breeding only with dogs and bitches which have not exhibited any signs.

The Rupniaks have recently imported an American Champion from Vicky Teshera of the Sheng

Li Kennels. This is Am. Ch. Sheng Li Mon Ju Copious, a son of CSPCA, AKC and Int. Ch. Sags Mtn. High Red Express who has sired eleven American Champions. Known by the name of 'Koko', the American import came out of quarantine in May 1994 and immediately started to win well in the UK showring. He has a short brush coat in red fawn, a "massive head", tight curl-back ears, excellent eyes and a scissor bite. Linda feels that Koko will add just what she needs to her kennel to produce type, quality and health, for his breeder had guaranteed him to be free of Hock Syndrome. His litter brother, Dormons Trail Blazer, also carries his AKC Championship title, and Am. Ch. Dormons Chin Ho, a full brother by a previous mating, owned by Shirley and Larry Rafferty, took Best of Breed at Westminster in 1993.

Also arriving at the Konishiki kennel in 1994, and in whelp at the time of import, was Sheng Li Burgundy, a grand-daughter of Red Express and daughter of CSPCA and AKC Ch. Meiting Luv Wun MacMurfee. She produced a healthy litter of six puppies, born in quarantine.

DAWNE BULLEN: SALTROCK

Dawne Bullen, living in Wales, purchased her first two Shar Pei, Shin-Soo and Tai Chi, as eight-week-old puppies in 1988. In February of 1989 a male, called 'Beamish', arrived at the Saltrock kennel. Interestingly, Dawne felt that she learned little from the information obtained in books and, instead, drew on her experience of farming and breeding and showing Persian cats. She believes in homoeopathy for her dogs and does not agree with inoculating them, for she considers this has caused problems in stock which she has sold. This is something which will be discussed again, later in this book.

Shin-Soo and Beamish were mated and produced the first litter of Saltrock puppies in February, 1990. In May of that year Tai-Chi whelped the first of her two litters in her short but happy life. A male from this litter, when mated to Ho-Choy, a bitch from the first Saltrock litter, produced

Dawne Bullen's Saltrock Yimsek, pictured at five months.

Photo courtesy: Dawne Bullen.

Saltrock Yimsek, known as 'Beasley', and it is he who has won most for Dawne. Beasley has since been mated back to Shin-Soo. Apparently the Saltrock Shar Pei love nothing better than speeding off across the heather on the Black Mountains in pursuit of wild rabbits and pheasants, though to date they have not managed to actually catch anything. They also have an avid dislike of cows, but tolerate sheep.

SUSAN STEAD

Susan Stead, though not an affix holder, has been kind enough to share some of the problems she has experienced, and these will be found in a later chapter. One of her Shar Pei, which did a good deal of winning, was Susan's first, Wrinkle Silkskin of Well, known as 'Esta' and bred by Angela Norman-Smith. Esta won the Shar Pei Club of GB's points trophy for bitches in 1988 and won both Best of Breed and Best Opposite Sex awards at championship level. Unfortunately, Esta's two litters of puppies both faded, and none have survived.

The Danish import, China House Mamma Jennifer, known as 'Bliss' was released from quarantine in April of 1992 and she, too, achieved some very satisfactory wins in the show ring. The most rewarding, and certainly the one which will go down in the breed's historical records, is that she was the very first Shar Pei to win Reserve in the Utility Group at a Championship Show. This great win came at Border Union on June 20th 1993, with James Peat judging the breed and Dennis Coxall the group. Luckily we are able to reproduce a photo taken on that wonderful day but sadly, only ten days later, Bliss was in renal failure, suffering from Swollen Hock Syndrome. Susan hopes that one day she will be lucky enough to have another Shar Pei which enjoys Bliss's good looks combined with good health.

Susan Stead with her Danish import China House Mamma Jennifer: Best of Breed and Reserve in the Utility Group at the Border Union Championship Show in 1993. Photo: Dave Freeman.

Myojo Christmas Cracker, owned by Wendy Coates.

Photo courtesy: Wendy Coates.

WENDY COATES: MYOJO

Wendy Coates (formerly Shrimpton) of the Myojo kennel had wonderful success at Cruft's in 1994, when she took both the bitch Challenge Certificate, with Myojo Christmas Tree, and the Dog Challenge Certificate and Best of Breed, with Taiyattang Chick-Weed at Myojo. Born on October 11th 1990, he was three years old. Sadly Chick's success in the show-ring was short-lived, as he met with a dreadful accident on April 14th 1994, less than five weeks after his achievement at Cruft's. Wendy has agreed that the unfortunate incident, and Chick's remarkable recovery, can be put into print, for it may give heart to anyone else who has the misfortune to have a similar experience.

Chick was walking with 'Kisser' in the local park and both ran up a forty foot railway embankment. Due to the wind blowing, it was obvious that neither had heard Wendy's calls. She climbed to the top, only to discover Chick lying between the railway tracks, some sixty to seventy yards further up, obviously having been dragged by a train. Chick's right front leg was severed above the pastern, the left front leg was broken and ripped from toes to elbow and, on this foot, he had lost two toes. His right hind leg was dislocated and his bottom was ripped from two inches along his tail, through his anus and down to his testicles. The following morning Chick underwent five hours of surgery, with two vets working on him. The X-rays showed that no other damage had been sustained, otherwise, Wendy says, she would not have given the go-ahead for attempts to be made to save him.

The vets cannot believe Chick's resilience to this trauma which, they believe, would have killed another dog. His recovery programme went through various stages. At first he would not relieve himself in front of people, so he had to be left for about ten minutes until he had finished. He also growled at Stella Chadwick, with whom he was very familiar, for each time he saw her it was when she was helping Wendy to lift him outside or to go to the vet's, so he associated her with moving him about. (Now he loves her.) At first he was moved every two hours to stop any fluid build-up in the lungs and to stop pressure sores. For the first three days he cried if Wendy left the room, so she became a hermit in the sitting-room. The next stage came about five days after the operation, when Chick wanted feeding. This lasted about a week. In the next stage he urinated on the carpet whenever Wendy left him to see her other dogs, or to go to work.

Myojo Christmas Tree: Bitch CC winner at Crufts 1994.

Photo courtesy: Wendy Coates.

With the aid of a harness, Chick has learned to walk again, at first leaning on Wendy but now doing it all on his own, and cocking his leg nearly as well as he did before the accident. Visits to the vet have changed dramatically; now Chick is quite 'cocky' about going there! Having made such a good recovery, Chick was even allowed to mate a bitch a few weeks after the accident. He now runs to the gate, in readiness to go out, every time he hears car keys. It is gratifying to know that his temperament has not changed at all – he still loves to see people!

DEVELOPMENT OF THE BREED

Breeders in England, like those in the USA, suffered in the breed's formative years from a lack of background information regarding ancestry. There was, as might have been expected, a great variation in type, but already the Shar Pei is beginning to look more uniform in the show-ring.

Although the first Shar Pei had come into the UK in 1981, there were no registrations for that year, but there were fourteen in 1982, these dogs being owned by four different people. There was so much interest in the breed that there was already a waiting list for puppies, so it was felt that such enthusiasm had been generated that it was time to try to form a breed club. An inaugural meeting was held in April 1983, but the first years were not easy ones, and it took a further four years of regular applications to the Kennel Club before the Chinese Shar-Pei Club of Great Britain was officially recognised, in 1987.

But things had really started to move ahead following the first Annual General Meeting in June 1984, when it was decided that the proposed club should produce its own newsletter. This was called 'The Wrinkle' and first published in 1984, providing a central link for members of the club.

Despite the fact that the proposed club had not, at that time, been recognised by the Kennel Club, it was already very active and held not only 'fun days' but also, in November 1984, the first of a number of educational seminars. I understand that, as the breed grew in strength and numbers, many exhibitors were not happy with the judges' interpretations of the breed standard, so an extended and illustrated standard was compiled and issued in the summer of 1988, with the aim of circulating it to those who were scheduled to, or likely to, judge the breed.

Entries at shows grew steadily through the late 1980s and by 1990 the Shar Pei had its own classes scheduled at Cruft's, as well as at other major Championship shows.

Once the Kennel Club had finally approved the breed's application for registration of a breed club, it meant that permission could be applied for to hold an Open show. So it was that the UK's first Shar Pei breed Open Show was held in conjunction with the Rare Breeds Spectacular in September 1987. A great success in so many ways, the show brought in an entry of one hundred and eighteen, made up from sixty-five exhibits. In 1990 the show was held on its own, with an entry of one hundred and fifty-three from eighty-nine Shar Pei.

I have already mentioned that fun days have been held, primarily for the benefit of owners of pet Shar Pei and, indeed, the club tries hard not to neglect those who do not campaign their dogs at shows. There is an annual dinner, held at Christmas-time, and a helpline service, so that those who encounter any sort of problem with their Shar Pei may contact someone for advice, a valuable service appreciated by many. As in America, the club has a Code of Ethics, which was drawn up in its original form in 1985. Many who are active in the breed are hopeful that Challenge Certificates will be offered to Shar Pei by the Kennel Club in the not-too-distant future; others think that the breed needs to stabilise still further before this day approaches.

The proposed Midland Shar Pei Club celebrated its second anniversary in March 1994, although it is still seeking registration with the English Kennel Club. The club has already issued some very informative magazines, and its own Code of Ethics, and it boasts an impressive record of events and activities. The club's philosophy is one of friendship and co-operation between all members, and it is dedicated to developing the image of the Shar Pei through improving knowledge. It has established 'helplines' at a regional level, as well as having an active welfare section.

THE SHAR PEI IN OTHER COUNTRIES

The Shar Pei is now found in many countries throughout the world but not, usually, in any great numbers. At the time of writing this book, the Shar Pei is not eligible for registration with Sweden's Kennel Club, but it is eligible in other parts of Scandinavia, so it will be interesting to follow developments now that the quarantine regulations have changed.

In Germany the breed appears to be strong, with the names of Joachim Weinberg and Linda Reinelt known in many other parts of the world. It was Joachim Weinberg who, in 1978, imported the first Shar Pei to Europe, these being Bedlam's Lover Boy and Bedlam's Love Song, both bred by Ellen Weathers Debo. These two Shar Pei were to become the first European champions, winning their respective categories at an International Show, in Luxembourg, in March 1980. The Weinberg/Reinelt partnership also imported Down-Homes Cream Zulu from Matgo Law's kennel in Hong Kong.

The breed certainly has a following in other parts of Europe and in Australia. It has been in the Philippines since 1980 and in Hawaii since as early as 1970. The first litter of Shar Pei to be whelped in South America was in 1982. Onyx Coale, of Wrinkles Unlimited, has carried out the first Artificial Insemination on a Shar Pei bitch in New Zealand, where she also takes her dogs into the classroom to teach children about the breed. Jenny Hart and Moira Sutherland started up a breed club in New Zealand a few years ago, despite the fact that numbers of Shar Pei there are still very limited. Jenny warns Shar Pei owners who live in sheep country to take care, as her own, and those belonging to other enthusiasts of the breed in New Zealand, have escaped and attacked sheep. She says how shocked she was by the damage that was done and, though her own only attacked one animal, it is common for dogs to attack several, leaving their victims to die from their injuries and from shock. She cautions people with a lot of stock to think twice before purchasing a Shar Pei, as she feels that the problem of sheep attacks by Shar Pei is more than just an isolated case.

In Hong Kong and Taiwan, Shar Pei enthusiasts are strong in number and Bob Brampton has judged the breed in the Far East, so I am most grateful to him for sharing with me his first-hand experiences. In Hong Kong it would appear that the Shar Pei being shown are similar to those found in the UK, but in Taiwan there seems to be more skin and consequent wrinkle, both in puppies and adults. This can make it difficult sometimes to find the eyes. They seem, generally, to have more bulk and are heavier in bone. Nelson Lam is making great efforts to educate people about the breed, and Frankie Law is also greatly involved.

The Hong Kong Shar Pei Club has recently been recognised by the Hong Kong Kennel Club, and it is Hong Kong that seems to have had most influence on the breed in Japan. Bob Brampton has also seen and judged the breed in Lithuania where he considers the Shar Pei to be of similar style to those in England, but with more substance.

How fascinating it will be, over the decades ahead, to see the Shar Pei mature throughout the world!

Chapter Five

THE BREED STANDARDS

ENGLISH KENNEL CLUB STANDARD (Interim)

GENERAL APPEARANCE
Alert, active, compact, short coupled, squarely built. Dogs larger and more powerful than bitches.

CHARACTERISTICS
Loose skin, frowning expression.

TEMPERAMENT
Calm, independent, very affectionate, and devoted to people.

HEAD & SKULL
Rather large in proportion to body, skull flat, broad, moderate stop. Fine wrinkles on forehead and cheeks continuing to form dewlaps. Muzzle distinctive feature of breed: moderately long, broad from eyes to point of nose without any suggestion of tapering. Lips and top of muzzle well padded causing slight bulge at base of nose. When viewed from front, bottom jaw appears wider than top due to padding of lips. Nose large, wide, preferably black but any colour conforming to general coat colour permissible.

EYES
Dark, medium size, almond shaped with frowning expression. Lighter colour permissible in cream and light fawn dogs. Function of eyeball or lid in no way disturbed by surrounding skin, folds or hair. Any sign of irritation of eyeball, conjunctiva or eyelids highly undesirable. Free from entropion.

EARS
Very small, rather thick, equilaterally triangular in shape, slightly rounded at tip, with tips pointing towards eyes. Set well forward over eyes, wide apart and close to skull. Pricked ears highly undesirable.

MOUTH
Bluish-black tongue preferred, pink spotted permissible. Solid pink tongue undesirable. Flews, roof of mouth and gums preferably black, lighter colours permissible in cream and light fawn. Teeth strong, with a perfect, regular and complete scissor bite, i.e. the upper teeth

closely overlapping the lower teeth and set square to the jaws. Padding of lower lip should not be so excessive as to interfere with the bite.

NECK
Short, strong, full; set well on shoulders, with loose skin under neck.

FOREQUARTERS
Shoulders muscular, well laid and sloping. Forelegs straight, moderate length, good bone; pasterns slightly sloping, strong and flexible.

BODY
Chest broad and deep, underline rising slightly under loin; back short, strong; topline dips slightly behind withers then rises over short, broad loin. Excessive skin on body when mature highly undesirable.

HINDQUARTERS
Muscular, strong; moderately angulated; hocks well let down.

FEET
Moderate size, compact, toes well knuckled. Fore and hind dew-claws may be removed.

TAIL
Rounded, narrowing to fine point, base set very high. May be carried high and curved; carried in tight curl; or curved over. Lack of tail highly undesirable.

GAIT/MOVEMENT
Free, balanced, vigorous.

COAT
Distinctive feature of breed. Short and bristly; harsh to touch. Straight and off-standing on body, generally flatter on limbs. No undercoat. Over 2.5 cms (1 inch) long undesirable. Never trimmed.

COLOUR
Solid colours – black, red, light or dark shades of fawn and cream. Frequently shaded on tail and back of thighs with lighter colour; patched white or spotted undesirable.

SIZE
46-51 cms (18-20 ins) at withers.

FAULTS
Any departure from the foregoing points should be considered a fault and the seriousness with which the fault should be regarded should be in exact proportion to its degree.

NOTE
Male animals should have two apparently normal testicles fully descended into the scrotum.

Reproduced by kind permission of the English Kennel Club.

AMERICAN KENNEL CLUB STANDARD

GENERAL APPEARANCE

An alert, dignified, active, compact dog of medium size and substance, square in profile, close-coupled, the well proportioned head slightly but not overly large for the body. The short, harsh coat, the loose skin covering the head and body, the small ears, the "hippopotamus" muzzle shape and the high-set tail impart to the Shar Pei a unique look peculiar to him alone. The loose skin and wrinkles covering the head, neck and body are superabundant in puppies but these features may be limited to the head, neck and withers in the adult.

SIZE, PROPORTION, SUBSTANCE

The preferred *height* is 18 to 20 inches at the withers. The preferred weight is 40 to 55 pounds. The dog is usually larger and more square bodied than the bitch but both appear well proportioned. *Proportion* - The height of the Shar Pei from the ground to the withers is approximately equal to the length from the point of breast-bone to the point of rump.

HEAD

Large, slightly but not overly, proudly carried and covered with profuse wrinkles on the forehead continuing into side wrinkles framing the face. *Eyes* – Dark, small, almond-shaped and sunken, displaying a scowling expression. In the dilute colored dogs the eye color may be lighter. *Ears* – extremely small, rather thick, equilateral triangles in shape, slightly rounded at the tips, edges of the ear may curl. Ears lie flat against the head, are set wide apart and forward on the skull, pointing toward the eyes. The ears have the ability to move. Pricked ears are a disqualification. *Skull* – Flat and broad, the stop moderately defined. *Muzzle* – One of the distinctive features of the breed. It is broad and full with no suggestion of snipiness. (The length from nose to stop is approximately the same as from stop to occiput.) *Nose* – Large and wide and darkly pigmented, preferably black but any color nose conforming to the general coat color of the dog is acceptable. In dilute colors, the preferred nose is self-colored. Darkly pigmented cream Shar Pei may have some light pigment either in the centre of their noses or on their entire nose. The lips and top of muzzle are well padded and may cause a slight bulge at the base of the nose.

TONGUE, ROOF OF MOUTH, GUMS AND FLEWS

Solid bluish-black is preferred in all colors except in dilute colors, which have a solid lavender pigmentation. A spotted tongue is a major fault. A solid pink tongue is a disqualification. (Tongue colors may lighten due to heat stress; care must be taken not to confuse dilute pigmentation with a pink tongue.) *Teeth* – strong, meeting in a scissors bite. Deviation from a scissors bite is a major fault.

NECK, TOPLINE, BODY

Neck – medium length, full and set well into the shoulders. There are moderate to heavy folds of loose skin and abundant dewlap about the neck and throat. The *topline* dips slightly behind the withers, slightly rising over the short, broad loin. *Chest* – broad and deep with the brisket extending to the elbow and rising slightly under the loin. *Back* – short and close-coupled. *Croup* – flat, with the base of the tail set extremely high, clearly exposing an uptilted anus. The high set *tail* is a characteristic feature of the Shar Pei. The tail is thick and round

BASIC ANATOMY OF THE SHAR PEI

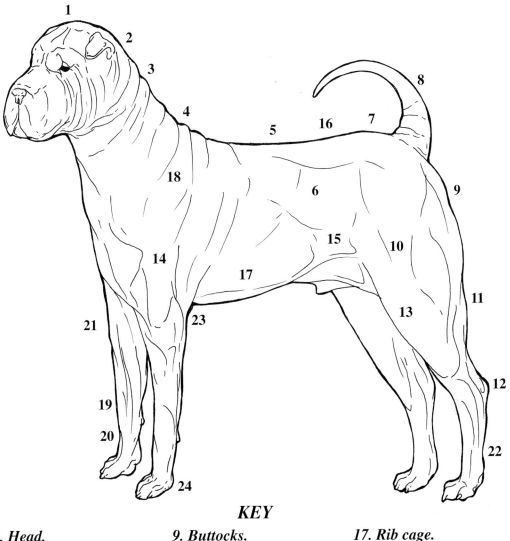

KEY

1. Head.
2. Nape of neck.
3. Collar (or crest).
4. Withers.
5. Back.
6. Coupling.
7. Croup.
8. Tail.

9. Buttocks.
10. Upper thigh.
11. Lower thigh.
12. Hock.
13. Stifle.
14. Upper arm.
15. Flank.
16. Loin.

17. Rib cage.
18. Shoulder.
19. Wrist.
20. Pastern.
21. Forearm.
22. Rear Pastern.
23. Elbow.
24. Foot

at the base, tapering to a fine point and curling over to either side of the back. The absence of a complete tail is a disqualification.

FOREQUARTERS

Shoulders – muscular, well laid back and sloping. *Forelegs* – when viewed from the front, straight, moderately spaced, with elbows close to the body. When viewed from the side, the forelegs are straight, the pasterns are strong and flexible. The bone is substantial but never heavy and is of moderate length. Removal of front dewclaws is optional. *Feet* – moderate in size, compact and firmly set. Not splayed.

HINDQUARTERS

Muscular, strong, and moderately angulated. The metatarsi (hocks) are short, perpendicular to the ground and parallel to each other when viewed from the rear. Hind dewclaws must be removed. Feet as in front.

COAT

The extremely harsh coat is one of the distinguishing features of the breed. The coat is absolutely straight and offstanding on the main trunk of the body but generally lies somewhat flatter on the limbs. The coat appears healthy without being shiny or lustrous. Acceptable coat lengths may range from extremely short "horse coat" up to the "brush coat", not to exceed one inch in length at the withers. A soft coat, a wavy coat, a coat in excess of one inch in length at the withers or a coat that has been trimmed is a major fault. The Shar Pei is shown in its natural state.

COLOR

Only solid colors are acceptable. A solid colored dog may have shading, primarily darker down the back and on the ears. The shading must be variations of the same body color (except in sables) and may include darker hairs throughout the coat. The following colors are a disqualifying fault: Not a solid color, i.e. Albino; Brindle; Parti-colored (patches); Spotted (including spots, ticked or roaning); Tan-pointed Pattern (including typical black and tan or saddled patterns).

GAIT

The movement of the Shar Pei is to be judged at a trot. The gait is free and balanced with the feet tending to converge on a centre line of gravity when the dog moves at a vigorous trot. The gait combines good forward reach and a strong drive in the hindquarters. Proper movement is essential.

TEMPERAMENT

Regal, alert, intelligent, dignified, lordly, scowling, sober and snobbish, essentially independent and somewhat standoffish with strangers, but extreme in his devotion to his family. The Shar-Pei stands firmly on the ground with a calm confident stature.

MAJOR FAULTS

1. Deviation from a scissors bite.
2. Spotted Tongue.
3. A soft coat, a wavy coat, a coat in excess of one inch in length at the withers or a coat that has been trimmed.

DISQUALIFICATIONS
Pricked Ears.
Solid Pink Tongue.
3. Absence of a complete tail.
4. Not a solid color, i.e. Albino; Brindle; Parti-colored (patches); Spotted (including spots, ticked or roaning); Tan-pointed Pattern (including typical black and tan or saddled patterns).

Reproduced by kind permission of the American Kennel Club. Approved October 8, 1991.

VARIATIONS IN STANDARDS
As can be expected with a breed which, though possessing an ancient history, is still on its way to reaching maturity throughout the world, there are several different Breed Standards currently in use. This can, undoubtedly, lead to confusion, especially when the breed is judged by a person from another country who is more conversant with a different Standard.

In Canada, to cite a clear example, the Breed Standard wording for Weight and Size reads: "40-51cm (15-20 ins) at withers. Dogs larger than bitches and more square. The equilibrium of individual proportions is very important." We can see from this that a Shar Pei which is three inches smaller than those at the lower end of the breed Standard specifications in Great Britain, or the USA, is acceptable in Canada. The Canadian Standard for the Shar Pei is not so specific about colour, allowing somewhat more latitude. It reads: "Colour: Black, smokey, dark brown, beige and cream, varying range of colour is seldom seen. Shaded on tail and back thighs with lighter colour, but without white patches or spotted."

It will therefore be appreciated that the comments I make with regard to the various features of the breed are open to slightly differing interpretations, depending upon which of the Shar Pei breed Standards one refers to. As far as possible, I have highlighted the major differences found between the American and English Standards, bearing in mind always that the latter is considerably more concise.

ANALYSIS AND INTERPRETATION

GENERAL APPEARANCE
Let us, first of all, consider general appearance which, in the English Standard, is limited to just a few words. 'Squarely built' gives the reader an instant picture of the outline required and ties in with the reference to a short loin in a later section of the English Standard and to "close-coupled" in the American one. An apt description of the Shar Pei is that of a warrior, standing four-square, with a certain calmness, yet showing determination. A comparison of dog to bitch is incorporated in this section of the English Standard, though it is detailed separately in the USA. In England the dog is to be larger and more powerful than the bitch. In the USA the dog is not only usually larger but also more square, though both sexes must be well proportioned. In many breeds, slightly greater length of loin is accepted in bitches than in dogs, due to their prospective maternal duties.

TEMPERAMENT
The temperament of the Shar Pei is well balanced and, undoubtedly, these dogs are devoted to their owners. However, being independent dogs, like many of the Asian breeds they can be somewhat aloof with strangers, though this is not mentioned in the breed Standards. They should have a calm temperament and, although they are not by any means aggressive dogs, they are

natural household guardians. I feel it is always important to cast one's mind back to the history of the breed and, in the case of the Shar Pei, to remember that it was used as a fighting dog. It is believed not to be a born fighter, but a breed which will enjoy fighting if encouraged to do so when very young. This is of great importance when bringing up a puppy and it is essential to emphasise that young Shar Pei, especially males, should be taught good manners from an early age. The majority of Shar Pei live very happily as household members and, provided that they are correctly disciplined from youth, they are the best of company.

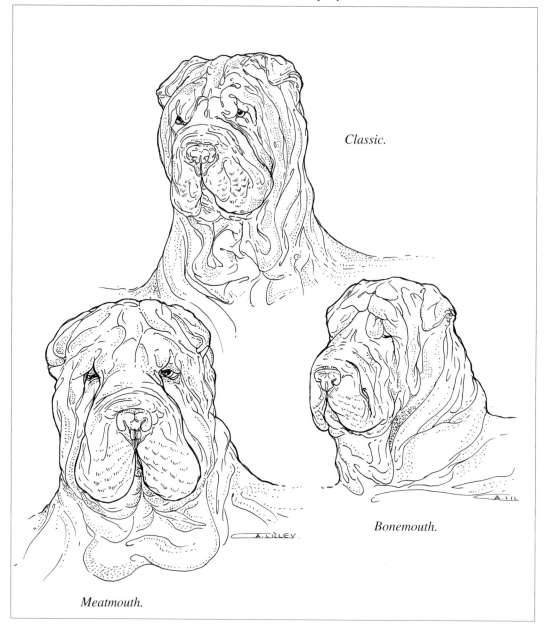

Classic.

Bonemouth.

Meatmouth.

HEAD

The Shar Pei is described by many as a 'head breed', the head being such a distinctive part of its anatomy. What can confuse those who are not entirely conversant with the Shar Pei is that there are varying head types and that more than one is acceptable.

A good head is a really distinctive feature of the breed. Those which are too snipey, too heavy or heavily wrinkled, or even 'Boxer-like' with over-large ears, stand out as being untypical and should be duly penalised. There is always a danger that, due to the heavy wrinkling in a puppy, a

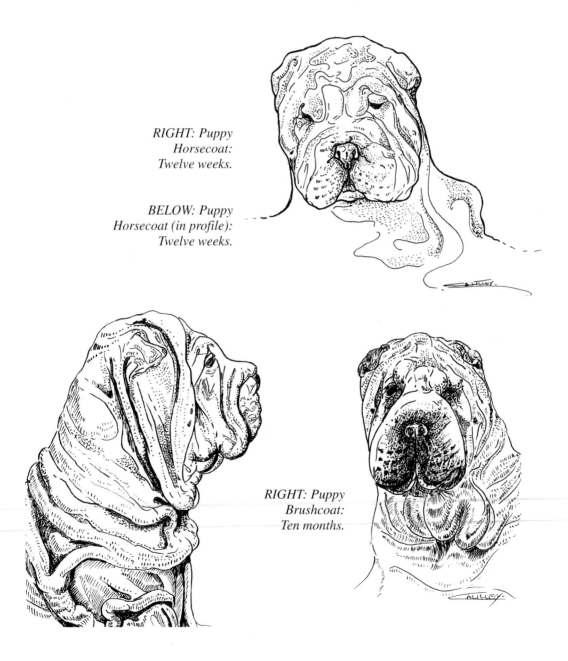

RIGHT: Puppy Horsecoat: Twelve weeks.

BELOW: Puppy Horsecoat (in profile): Twelve weeks.

RIGHT: Puppy Brushcoat: Ten months.

Taiyattangs The Power of One: This puppy has a Bonemouth head type, and a frowning expression, which is much sought-after in China. Photo: Bill Lilley.

Although this Shar Pei is pictured squinting into the sunlight, he is too heavy and 'Mastiff-looking'. Photo: Bill Lilley.

This dog has a very heavy 'hippo-type' muzzle. A good bite would not be expected from this type of head.

Photo courtesy: Bill Lilley.

breeder may overlook the structure of the bone shape underneath and, when the wrinkles lessen with adulthood, an incorrect skull-shape is found beneath. In cases where there is too much wrinkling the same may apply, but the optical illusion is that the head is too large for the body, often this being due to over-profuse skin and consequent wrinkling.

In a correct head one should find a slight stop, though viewed from the side the stop looks more apparent than it actually is, due to prominence of wrinkle on the brow. In proportion the length of muzzle, from tip of nose to stop, should be roughly the same as from stop to occiput. The description used in the American Standard, of the muzzle being the shape of that of a hippopotamus, conjures up a vivid picture and it is clear, from this, that the bottom jaw appears wider than the top, due to padding. Whilst a black nose is preferable, other colours are acceptable, provided that they conform to the coat colour.

The three head shapes which are acceptable are, most usually, described as the 'Classic', the 'Meatmouth' and the 'Bonemouth', good examples of the last not being easy to find.

The Classic head is moderately heavy and full, with solid structure beneath the heavy padding, giving a rounded appearance to the muzzle. Because the padding is dense, there is an appearance of a larger head, but this should not appear excessively so. In the Classic head there is some variety in the amount of bulge at the point at which the nose joins the muzzle.

The underlying bone structure of the Meatmouth is the same as that of the Classic head, the difference being that the padding over the bone is much heavier. This gives more of the 'hippopotamus' effect and a rather large head, though the head must never be so large that it upsets the overall balance of the Shar Pei.

A head which is more difficult to find is the Bonemouth, in which the strength of muzzle depends on the underlying bone structure, rather than on the padding, which is somewhat lighter than in the two heads mentioned above. Because of the underlying structure, the power of the muzzle in the Bonemouth does not diminish with age.

EYES

The eye of the Shar Pei has been the cause of some anxiety, and eye problems will be dealt with in a later chapter. Let us here concern ourselves with the correct shape of the eye, which is the shape of an almond. A major difference between the American and English Standards is that the former calls for a small eye which is sunken and the latter for a medium-sized eye, stipulating that its function should not be disturbed in any way. Indeed, the English Standard even goes so far as to say that signs of irritation are highly undesirable and that the eye should be free from entropion. Such comment, I feel, is an indication that British breeders have recognised some of the problems which the Shar Pei can encounter and are doing their best to eliminate them. The American Standard asks for a scowling expression and, whilst both Standards require a dark eye, provision is made for a lighter eye in Shar Pei with lighter coloured coats.

EARS

The ears should be very small in comparison to the size of the head and should be rather thick. It is interesting that the Canadian Standard says that: "In some dogs, the ears are as big as the thumb finger-nail and cover the auricular canal." In shape they are triangular but slightly rounded at the tips, which point in the direction of the eyes. They are to be set well forward over the eyes, though wide apart, and they should lie close to the skull. A pricked ear is highly undesirable in England and a disqualification in the USA. In the American Standard, the edges of the ear are allowed to curl. The Shar Pei has an ability to move its ears at will but, when they hear noise, they will usually snap back into position.

This six-month-old puppy is showing even teeth and a good bite. Photo: Carol Ann Johnson.

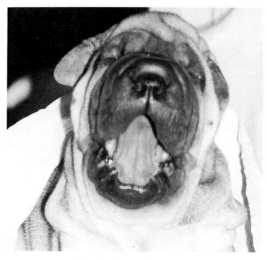

Displaying a lavender/lilac tongue. Photo: Bill Lilley.

MOUTH

The mouth of the Shar Pei is required to have a scissor bite, with the upper teeth closely overlapping the lower ones, and the American Standard points out that any deviation from this is a major fault. A condition known as 'tight-lip' is when the lower lip rolls up and over the lower teeth. In many cases the lip is very tight and it is virtually impossible to roll it down sufficiently to show the bite. Clearly, such a condition makes it difficult for the Shar Pei to eat and, in time, there is a chance that the lip will actually push back the lower teeth, causing an overshot bite. The teeth should be strong and there should be six incisors between the canine teeth. In some cases the canines are recurved and this should not be penalised, because the reason for it can be traced back in history (see the HKKA Standard, Chapter Three: The Shar Pei in America).

TONGUE

The dark blue-black tongue is a feature of the breed and is to be preferred but, again, provision is made for latitude in Shar Pei with certain coat colours. This provision, however, differs considerably between America and England. In the USA a spotted tongue is a major fault, whilst in England a pink-spotted tongue (known also as a flowered tongue) is permissible. In some cases the slightly spotted tongue of a puppy will fill in with maturity. A solid pink tongue is not acceptable. It is essential that one does not confuse a lavender tongue (permissible in dilute colours) with a pink tongue, and note should be taken that the colour of the tongue is inclined to lighten with heat stress. Colour of the flews, roof of mouth and gums should ideally be black but, again, lighter colours are allowed for in lighter-coloured dogs.

NECK

The neck of the Shar Pei is another feature which differs according to the two breed Standards with which we now concern ourselves. In England it should be short and strong, whilst in America a medium length of neck is called for. Both require it to be full and well set into the shoulders.

There is loose skin and dewlap around the neck and throat and this can, of course, add to the appearance of a short neck.

FOREQUARTERS
A typical Shar Pei requires muscular shoulders which are not only well laid back but also sloping. Viewed from the front, the forelegs should be straight and the American Standard requires them to

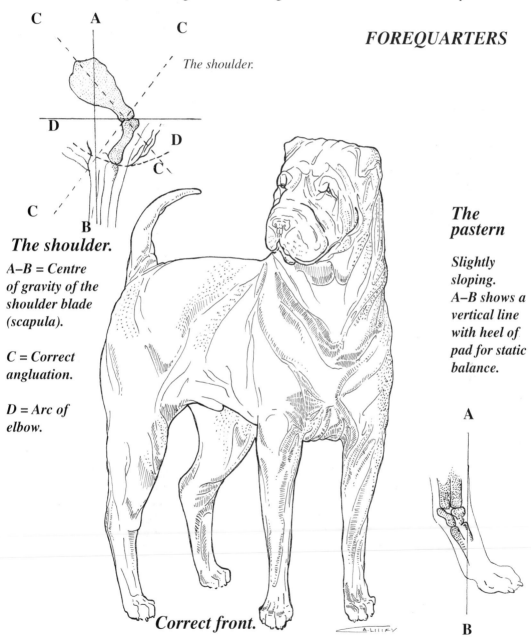

The shoulder.

FOREQUARTERS

The shoulder.

A–B = Centre of gravity of the shoulder blade (scapula).

C = Correct angluation.

D = Arc of elbow.

Correct front.

The pastern

Slightly sloping. A–B shows a vertical line with heel of pad for static balance.

be 'moderately spaced', indicating that they should be neither too close together nor too far apart. In a correct front, the feet should point straight forward though, over the years, there have been many who have considered that for the feet to point out very slightly (but not excessively) is acceptable. Clearly a loose elbow is not wanted but bone should be substantial, albeit not over-heavy. Moderate length of leg is called for and the strong, flexible pasterns are, in England, to be slightly sloping. Nonetheless, this is no excuse for a Shar Pei to stand like a rocking-horse, nor should its front bow.

BODY

Construction of the Shar Pei's body is not always fully understood, especially in relation to its topline, which is intended to dip slightly behind the withers and then rise slightly over the loin. The loin itself is to be short and broad, in keeping with the square outline of the dog. A broad,

Correct topline, dipping slightly behind the withers and rising slightly over the loin.

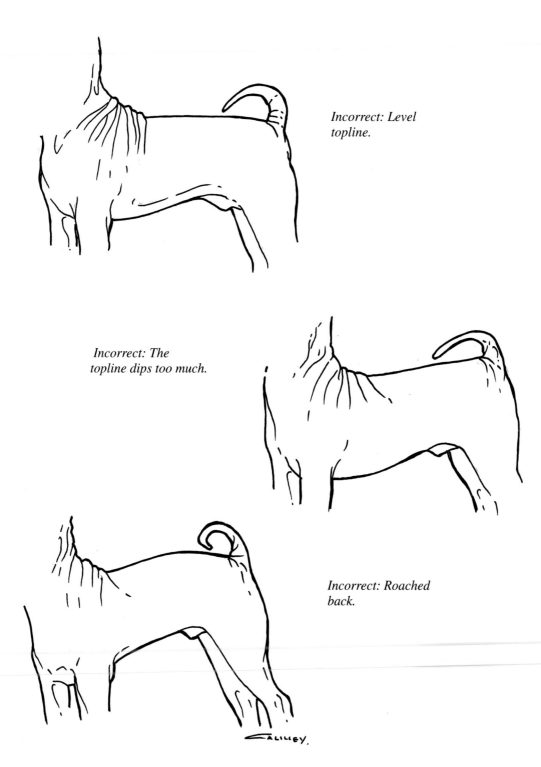

Incorrect: Level topline.

Incorrect: The topline dips too much.

Incorrect: Roached back.

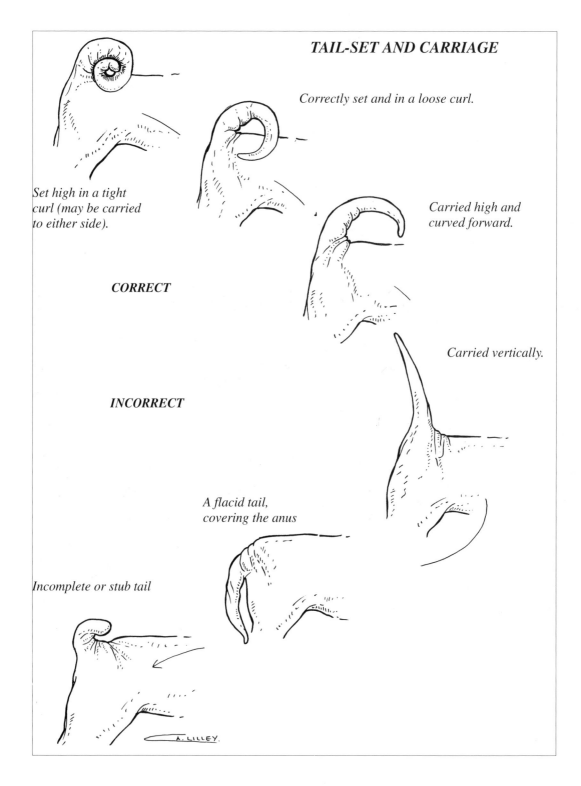

TAIL-SET AND CARRIAGE

Correctly set and in a loose curl.

Set high in a tight
curl (may be carried
to either side).

Carried high and
curved forward.

CORRECT

Carried vertically.

INCORRECT

A flacid tail,
covering the anus

Incomplete or stub tail

A. LILLEY.

deep chest is required, with a stipulation, in the American Standard, that the brisket should reach to the elbow and then, common to both Standards, rise slightly under the loin. The amount of wrinkle on an adult is important, as this is one of the features of the breed – again with an important function in the original specimen. Whilst excessive wrinkle is, in the English Standard at least, highly undesirable, too plain a body is also not to be encouraged.

TAIL

In America there is mention of the croup which should be flat and, common to both Standards, the tail set should be extremely high, in conjunction with which the anus will be at an up-tilted angle. The base of the tail is rounded and the tail then narrows to form a point. It may be carried in a variety of ways – curling over to either side of the back, in a tight curl or carried high and curved. Tails which are not acceptable are those which are too low set, and which, in consequence, are carried too low, sometimes curled and sometimes carried straight out in line with the back. Bob tails, those which are short and upright, are also incorrect, and no tail at all is highly undesirable – in America a disqualification.

Taiyattangs Gracelands: Top Puppy in Breed 1991, pictured at four months. The 'Chinese coin' tail is highly-prized in China.

Photo: Bill Lilley.

HINDQUARTERS

These should be strong, muscular and moderately angulated, a point on which both Standards entirely agree. Straightness of stifle, as in the Chow, is a serious fault and must be discouraged. The hocks, well let down, should be perpendicular and parallel when viewed from the rear. In England it is a matter of choice whether front and hind dewclaws are removed, but in the USA there is choice only on the forelegs, the hind dewclaws necessarily being removed. The compact, moderate-sized feet should have well-knuckled toes and should not be splayed.

Good rear angulation which will give overall balance and correct movement.

Incorrect: The straight stifles cause an imbalance to the body, which makes the topline dip too much. The dog is also out at elbow with a dippy front. Incorrect movement will result.

GAIT

The English Standard sums up gait in three short words: "free, balanced, vigorous". Whilst these words are descriptive, especially when one has borne in mind stipulations concerning fore and hindquarters and body, the American Standard is much more detailed, telling the reader that the Shar Pei is to be judged at a trot and that the feet tend to converge on a centre line of gravity when the dog is moved at a vigorous trot. In my opinion, this goes without saying in a moderately long-legged breed, but there is no harm in pointing it out, as there are those who do not expect this natural convergence, known as single-tracking, to occur! In the USA a good forward reach and strong drive from behind are called for, meaning that the dog can cover the ground quickly, and with minimum effort. As they rightly say: "Proper movement is essential."

LEFT: Kathy Kamakeeaina gaiting her home-bred Am. Ch. Maka Sy Snoodle in an American show ring. The American breed standard states that the Shar Pei should be moved at a trot.

Holloway

RIGHT: Taiyattang Chickweed at Myojo with owner/handler Wendy Coates winning Best of Breed at Crufts 1994. Photo courtesy: Wendy Coates.

COAT

Now that we have covered the anatomical aspects of the Shar Pei's breed Standards, we must move on to the vexed question of coat for, undoubtedly, there has been much debate concerning this aspect over the years. Let me refer you back again to the HKKC Standard, which gives a clear description of why a Shar Pei's coat should be harsh, namely that it should be "absolutely too uncomfortable to be held in any canine mouth." The coat is another particularly distinctive feature of the breed; it should be short, bristly and harsh to the touch. The shortest is termed a 'horse coat' and the longer coat, termed 'brush coat', should not exceed one inch (2.2 cms) in length. In the USA this maximum length is considered to be the maximum length of coat at the withers. Each strand of hair is to be absolutely straight, and is off-standing on the body but generally flatter on the limbs. The American Standard stipulates that soft and wavy coats are major faults and that the Shar Pei must be shown in its natural state and not be trimmed. This statement indicates that the soft long coat, which used to be favoured by some breeders in the USA, is clearly uncharacteristic and is therefore not to be encouraged. Undoubtedly, when other breeds have been used in re-developing and perfecting a breed such as the Shar Pei, 'throw-backs' will occur from time to time, but breeders should be aware that this might happen and should take the necessary steps not to allow dogs with undesirable features to be bred from. The name Shar Pei is said to mean 'sandy-coated dog' and this is relevant to the texture of the coat, not to the colour. It behoves dedicated breeders to keep it this way.

Konishiki Couch Potatoe and Konishiki Chocolate Chip: Brother and sister, pictured at five months old. The brush coat should not exceed one inch (2.5cm.) in length.

Photo courtesy: Linda Rupniak.

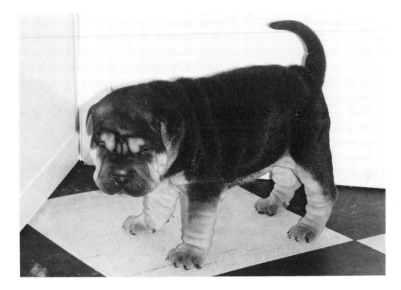

A black-and-tan bitch puppy, pictured at five weeks old. This colour is not accepted by the Kennel Clubs.

Photo: Bill Lilley.

COLOUR

In the Shar Pei this is complex, as is to be expected if breeds such as the Tibetan Mastiff, amongst others, have been employed in re-developing the breed. Indeed, from my studies of the Asian breeds over a number of years, I am now convinced that their colour genetics, in general, are probably more complex than those of any other canine group.

As with the long coats, unusual coat patterns will come through from time to time and breeders will have to learn to live with these. The Shar Pei is a relatively new breed in the West and, I feel certain, as the years move on, breeders will be surprised at how the predominant colours of the breed change. Solid colours are the only ones accepted and those included in the UK Standard are listed as black, red, light or dark shades of fawn and cream. However, "shading" is allowed, though the American Standard stipulates that the shading must be a variation of the body colour, except in sables, and that it may include darker hairs. Here, I feel, is the clue to the very fact that breeders will see colour changes develop with time, for sable coats are made up of an exceptionally complex set of genes and carry black in combination with other colours. Shading permissible in the UK is to be on the tail and back of thighs. In England patched white and spotted Shar Pei are undesirable, whilst in the USA albino, brindle, parti-colours and tan points, including typical black and tan or saddled patterns, are disqualifying faults.

DEFINITIONS OF COLOUR

Having covered the colour of the breed in relation to the Standards, I feel we should now look at the subject in more depth. In April 1980 Mr Matgo Law sent to the USA a more detailed description of the colours recognised in the breed in Hong Kong; these were taken into account and documented. The following precis of the findings will possibly be of help to enthusiasts and breeders who are interested in this aspect of the Shar Pei but, it must be stressed, not all colours found in the breed fall within the guidelines set down in the breed Standards.

Basic colours have black pigmentation, also known as charcoal. This is on the skin, nose, tongue, mouth/flews and pads of the feet. The nails, though, may be lighter.

Dilute colours have no black (charcoal) anywhere. The skin, nose and also the nails are self-coloured and blend with the coat colour. Eyes in dilutes may be light or dark and the tongue may vary from a light to a dark lavender.

Cream is an off-white colour and can variously be described as light cream, cream or dark cream. The ears may be darker and there can be shading along the dorsal line. In creams the nose is of a brick colour with a black rim. Eye colour should be deep brown and ideally the tongue should be completely blue-black. Cream dilute can also be found.

Fawn can range from a very light tan or golden colour, to a dark tan or golden. This has also been described as cinnamon. Again, there can be darker shading along the dorsal line. The nose and foot pads should be of a solid colour and the flesh-coloured noses of some whelps turn black within about a week. Red fawns can have skin, eyes and toe nails of a lighter colour.

Black may be a true black or with a blue, grey, brown or red tinge on the sides. The colour is uniform over the body, neck, head and legs with very little variation. When exposed to the sun for long periods such coats may fade to a rusty-grey colour.

Red can be from mahogany to rich chestnut red, such as the colour of an Irish Setter, and colour is uniform over body, neck, head and legs, again with very little variation. The nose should ideally be black. Five-point red dilutes vary from a distinct deep red fawn to a dark red with little variation of colour. The five points are the nose, eyes, skin, foot pads and anus.

Apricot is a dilute colour, similar to that of the five-point red dilute, but lighter. The colour is distinctly apricot and ranges in shade from light to dark.

Brown is a medium or dark brown colour, once again with little variation in colour on body, neck, head and legs.

Chocolate can vary in colour from medium to dark, such as the milk or dark chocolate which one can buy to eat. Colour, though, is uniform over body, neck, head and legs. The nose is also chocolate and the eyes usually of a yellowish hue. The tongue is light purple. The colour termed 'chocolate' includes liver, liver being of the same genetic make-up.

Sable coats have a lacing of black hairs over a lighter ground colour. The hairs themselves are of different colours, but not white. Once again there is little variation of colour over body, neck, head and legs. Sable dilute involves a lacing of darker hair over a lighter coloured ground. Again, the hairs are of separate colours but neither colour is white and there is little variation of colour over body, neck, head and legs.

Silver dilute is a bluish, silverish smoky colour. The term includes blue, grey and taupe (the colour of a mole). As with so many colours in the Shar Pei, there is little variation in colour over body, head, neck and legs. The nose is of a slate colour and the mouth and tongue are lavender. The skin, eyes, pads of feet and nails are self-coloured.

According to Matgo Law's detailed description of colours recognised in Hong Kong, sent to the USA in April of 1980, parti-colours, brindles and black and tans should be penalised and certainly not used in breeding programmes.

Other colours which are, therefore, recognised to exist but which are not solid colours are: Albino, in which there is no pigment either in coat or skin; Brindle, involving a mixture of black hairs with those of a lighter colour, usually in tan, brown or grey and displaying a typical 'tiger stripe' pattern; Parti-colour, in which two colours, one of which must be white, are broken up in more or less equal proportions; Spotted (sometimes referred to as 'flowered') with spots, ticks or roaning; and, finally, a Tan-pointed pattern, such as the colour commonly found in either a black and tan or liver and tan Dobermann, a saddle pattern such as that of the German Shepherd, or some other combination.

Chapter Six

CHOOSING A PUPPY

THE INITIAL DECISIONS

Before becoming the owner of a Shar Pei, you should consider the matter very carefully indeed. There will be many decisions to make, but the two major ones are whether or not you can and should own a dog, and whether or not a Shar Pei is the right breed for you and your immediate family members.

Only you can decide if you are the right person to own a dog, but what must be borne in mind is that a dog should remain with you for the duration of its life, not just for a few years, months or even weeks until the novelty wears off. Any dog needs to be housed, fed and cared for, which takes up considerable time and expense and, in my opinion, absolutely no dog should have to be left at home all day alone, whilst all family members are out at work or at school.

Provided you are satisfied that you can do a dog justice, let us now look at the many factors which have to be taken into account when deciding whether a Shar Pei is the right breed. Ownership of any dog, and a Shar Pei in particular, must be something which is agreed upon by the whole family. Of course, it is natural that different people have different preferences, but a Shar Pei is definitely not the right breed for you if, perhaps, one of your family simply does not like the breed and desperately wants, for example, a Toy breed. There is the chance that a Shar Pei would 'grow on' the reluctant household member, but there is a risk that always, at the back of that person's mind, would be the niggling feeling that a Toy breed would have been better. Shar Pei are intelligent dogs who may well pick up these vibrations and react to them.

Consider, too, whether or not the unusual texture of the Shar Pei's coat is likely to cause any irritation to the skin of anyone in the family. Does anyone suffer from allergies of any kind? If so, it is wise to arrange for that person to spend time in the close company of Shar Pei, to see whether or not there is any allergic reaction to the coat. Far better to discover such a problem before your purchase is made, rather than afterwards, when the dog may then, of necessity, have to be re-housed – a traumatic event for both dog and owners.

Another aspect which one must take into account is whether or not all members of the family are up to having a strong and sizable dog in their environment. If there are any elderly, infirm relatives living with you, could they cope, or could arrangements be made so that the Shar Pei did not, inadvertently, bump into them? The same applies to children in the house.

We have already touched upon some of the bad publicity the breed has had in the press and only you, as a new owner, can decide whether you and your children will be sensible enough to bring up a Shar Pei properly so that nobody is ever harmed, albeit by accident. From a purely personal point of view, I never allow any puppies, of whatever breed, to go to homes where there are infants. Perhaps I am just over-cautious, *but small children can be unintentionally rough and, from*

CSPCA Ch. Hao Kan En Tse: Taking on a puppy is a big responsibility, and with a Shar Pei you must be prepared to cope with a fairly sizeable and powerful dog.

Vavna Photography.

a breeder's standpoint, I would rather be safe than sorry. Having said that, I know that there are Shar Pei owners and breeders who bring their children up with dogs and find that they mix exceptionally well. So much depends on the parents, and the way they teach their children to handle and to react to dogs. But to discuss this subject at length could soon become another book, so, suffice it to say, the ultimate decision has to rest with you.

MALE OR FEMALE?

Assuming, therefore, that you are as certain as you can be that a Shar Pei really is the breed you want to have sharing your life for a good few years to come, you would be wise to consider whether you feel a bitch or a dog would be best, before approaching breeders with your request. Dogs (males) are, usually, somewhat larger and stronger than bitches and may require rather more exercise. Whilst both sexes can be equally loyal and loving with their owners, male Shar Pei are often found to be more aggressive with intruders and uninvited guests. Many breeds of Asian origin do not welcome a stranger into the home until they are certain that that person has been accepted by the other family members. This is a point which is worthy of serious consideration from the outset.

There is also the question of breeding, with whichever sex you choose. Once again, perhaps I am a little conservative in my opinions, but I do not feel that one should ever approach a new breed with the aim of breeding from the first bitch owned. You will have to be sure, firstly, that she is likely to be a good brood bitch and, secondly, that, in maturity, she is sufficiently typical of the breed. A major problem, if you decide to have a bitch, will be that she comes in season (on heat) roughly every six or seven months. A season lasts about three weeks and, during this time, she will receive attention from male dogs, so it will be difficult to exercise her, except in isolated areas. If there are male dogs in your home, she will have to be kept well away from them. It is, of course, possible to spay a bitch (or indeed castrate a dog) but this should not be done until after her first season. Also, bear in mind that, under certain circumstances, a bitch cannot be shown if she has been spayed and has not whelped puppies registered with the country's Kennel Club. If you do decide that your pet bitch is eventually to be spayed, you will have to exercise her well and watch her diet, so that she does not gain excess weight.

A question which I have been asked many times is: "How do I find a bitch to which I can mate my dog?" If this question is in your mind, forget it! You do not decide to have a dog because you want him to be used at stud. Only his qualities in maturity will decide whether, or not, he is worthy of this and he should be of exceptionally high merit if he is eventually to be used. It is the bitch's owner who selects the most appropriate stud dog, and many a pet dog has been ruined by unwarranted use at stud. There are exceptions but, often, when a pet dog has been used at stud, even if only once, he will regularly mark his territory, which can be a great nuisance if he lives as a house pet. It is also likely that he will try to assert his authority over other males, which is not always an easy thing to cope with in a fairly heavy breed.

FINDING A BREEDER

So, having dealt with the pros and cons, let us now look at how best you can locate a breeder who is likely to be able to provide you with the Shar Pei of your choice. You will probably have already decided whether you want to own a Shar Pei simply as a pet or as a potential show dog, and you must make this clear to breeders from the outset. Most of those who breed typical stock either show their own dogs or are involved, in some capacity, with the show-world; this way they are well placed to assess the qualities of other Shar Pei and can decide what they might incorporate into their own breeding programmes. It has to be borne in mind that, in many countries, the Shar Pei is not a numerically strong breed and will not have specific classes scheduled in a show, so few, if any, Shar Pei will be present. However, there are shows in the UK, for example, which now regularly classify the Shar Pei as a separate breed and these draw good entries. Many general championship shows are, frequently, also well supported by Shar Pei owners in the Any Variety classes and, at some Open shows, it is possible occasionally to find a few Shar Pei. In the UK, the British Utility Breeds Open and Championship shows always classify the breed and there are usually good entries, as well as at breed club shows.

So, find out from the canine press which shows are likely to have Shar Pei entered and take yourself along, to meet breeders and exhibitors who will, hopefully, be able to give you good advice. To obtain a Shar Pei with breeding of your choice, you may have to go on a waiting list, but this will be worthwhile. Far better to wait for the kind of Shar Pei to which you are most attracted, than to buy one which is totally different. Bear in mind that, at this early stage in the breed's re-development, Shar Pei vary considerably, according to the bloodlines behind them.

Occasionally Shar Pei puppies are advertised for sale in the canine or general press, but I would urge you to take extreme care. You will feel more confident that you are buying from a reputable breeder if you have already done at least some ground-work. Under no circumstances should you ever purchase a Shar Pei puppy from a pet shop, even if it is an expensive one. The puppy may look appealing, and you may feel you simply must give it a new, loving home; but put yourself in the position of a Shar Pei breeder for a moment. If you had brought up a litter of puppies with care, and watched them develop into little personalities over a number of weeks, wouldn't you like to know who was buying them?

Shar Pei are sold at various prices and, in a book of this nature, it would be imprudent to give

It takes an expert eye to assess the show potential of a young puppy. This pup grew up to be Heathstyle Mistletoe.
Photo courtesy: Dulcie Ligget.

any guide. However, do not expect your Shar Pei to be cheap. And remember, if you struggle in order to afford to buy one, you can probably not afford the upkeep and the veterinary bills which will arise, so perhaps you should, even at this stage, think again.

The age at which you buy your Shar Pei puppy will be stipulated largely by the breeder and a lot will depend on whether you require a Shar Pei for the show ring, or simply as a family pet. No puppy should change hands before the age of ten weeks, so, if you are offered one younger than that, I suggest you seek another breeder. If you want to show your Shar Pei, you will probably have to wait until the puppy is somewhat older, so that the breeder can be as sure as possible that the dog you are taking home with you will be a worthy show specimen. Many breeders like to wait until the age of five or six months before selling stock with show potential. Something else about which you should be on your guard is that, unless a dog has already been entered in shows and has won well – in which case the dog will be older and it is highly unlikely that the owner will want to part company anyway – no breeder can sell what they term a "show dog". The Shar Pei may have show potential, but all manner of things can go wrong during the dog's development, and so it is most unwise of breeders to use this term as freely as some do.

Do not be talked into buying more than one puppy, in the first instance. Whilst it is true that many dogs enjoy the company of others, if you are purchasing your very first Shar Pei, I suggest that you allow the puppy time to become accustomed to you as owners whilst, at the same time, you will learn a great deal from the Shar Pei in your care. If there are already other dogs in your home, you will need to have discussed the matter thoroughly with the breeder of the Shar Pei puppy. As a general rule, it is unwise to introduce a bumptious new puppy into the home if you have an old, infirm dog living with you. Perhaps you have facilities to keep them separate but, if not, you should be prepared to allow nature to take its course, to be fair to your older dog, before you buy a puppy. If you genuinely feel that your own set-up would allow your old dog still to be happy with a lively youngster in the home, you will need to exercise extreme caution when you do allow the two to meet. Never, under any circumstances, allow your old dog to feel in any way pushed out, or usurped. Always give that extra bit of attention to your dog, who has, after all, served you well for a good many years and deserves your care and affection until the very end.

ASSESSING A LITTER

So, let us assume that you have decided on the breeder from which you intend to buy your Shar Pei puppy, and that a litter is available. Some breeders will be happy for you to see the puppies during the early weeks of their life, but I do not recommend that breeders invite prospective purchasers to their homes until the puppies are, at least, starting to be weaned. Nothing must be allowed to worry the dam more than necessary whilst she is still feeding her litter. Should you be invited before the puppies are old enough to leave home, be sure you have not been in contact with a contagious canine disease, for the puppies will not yet have been vaccinated. Please do not rush up to the puppies, but wait until you are invited to do so, for it may be that the breeder does not wish you to touch them whilst they are so young, and the dam may still be protective. This is perfectly understandable, albeit disappointing for you, but you must comply with the breeder's wishes. Don't think, either, that you will necessarily be able to select the puppy of your choice. The breeder, who may also be an exhibitor, might not yet have made a decision about which of the puppies to retain. You may just have to be patient.

When you get into serious conversation with a breeder about purchasing a puppy, you should not be put off by the fact that you will probably be asked as many questions about yourself, and your environment, as you will wish to ask about the puppy. This is merely because a dedicated breeder, who is interested in the future of the puppies, will want to be sure they are going to suitable homes. In the course of conversation, you should be able to find out not only the merits of that particular breeder's bloodlines, but also any problems which are likely to be encountered. The Shar Pei is still in its early years of re-development and so any honest breeder should be willing to open up to you, just as you are expected to open up when questions are asked.

The time will come when the puppies are old enough to leave their dam and this may be your first chance to visit. It is important that you do not fall into the trap of buying a puppy if you are not thoroughly convinced that the litter has been well raised, and that the puppies are in good health and of a suitable quality. The outward signs of good health in a pet puppy should be the same as those of a puppy destined for the show ring. There is always a temptation to take one away to give it a 'better life'. Please don't be fooled. Purchase of a puppy from a less-than-reputable breeder just means that the litter will have been sold sooner than might otherwise have happened, so that yet another litter can be bred to find its way onto the 'puppy market'.

Everyone's home differs in such things as taste, but the puppies you see should be kept in a clean environment and, if they are allowed into the house, all the better. Particularly if you are buying a pet who will live in the house with you and your family, it will be of great advantage if the newcomer has seen the inside of a family home, rather than having spent the first weeks of life entirely in a kennel situation. You should be permitted to see the dam of the litter, possibly with her offspring, but it may well be that the sire is not available for you to see, for he might be owned by someone else and could, indeed, live many miles away. If the sire is, however, owned by the breeder you should ask to see him. If the dam is not available for you to see, please exercise extreme caution and thoroughly question the reason why. If you are absolutely convinced that the reason is genuine and valid, ask to see adult stock of similar breeding so that you know, very roughly, what the puppy you intend to buy is likely to grow up like.

This long-coated 'bear' puppy is absolutely delightful, but destined for a pet home rather than the show ring.
Photo courtesy: Linda Rupniak.

This puppy has an 'over-done' head; a good bite is unlikely to develop.
Photo: Bill Lilley.

POINTS TO LOOK FOR

A healthy puppy should look plump and well fed, though not excessively pot-bellied as this could be a sign of worms. A thin puppy could also indicate that worms are present but could, equally well, not have received adequate nourishment, or perhaps both. You would be unwise to select such a puppy or, at least, not without a thorough veterinary check up. Also take a note of the eyes. They should look bright and clear, and there should certainly be no discharge either from the eyes or from the nose. The coat will need to be inspected carefully, not just where it is visible but on the tummy, too, and inside the legs. There should be no sign of a rash and the coat should not have bare patches. There should certainly be no sores anywhere on the body, including between the wrinkles and on the toes. There should be absolutely no sign of fleas or other parasites. The puppy should not scratch excessively and it is wise to check that the insides of the ears are clean and free from discharge; there should certainly be no odour from the ear. Puppies go to the toilet frequently, so you may also have a chance to check that the puppy's motions are normal and not too runny, for this could indicate a problem which might be more than just an upset tummy. Be sure that the puppy you hope to buy is fully alert, aware of noises, and does not appear to be lethargic, excessively aggressive with the siblings or, indeed, overly shy with you.

Depending on how much experience you have had with dogs and, perhaps more importantly, with Shar Pei, you may or may not know what to look for, in terms of construction, at this early stage in the puppy's development. This means that you will probably have to be guided, to a

This four-month-old, heavily-boned puppy shows how the weight of the heavy jowls and padding can pull down the bottom eyelids. This improves with age, but this pup is better suited to a pet home rather than the show ring.

Photo: Bill Lilley.

certain extent, by the breeder. As a general rule, you might be well advised to have a puppy which is pretty much average in size in relation to its siblings, for one which is either very large, or very small, may not turn out to be as typical of the breed as the others. The feet and bones will already look somewhat out of proportion to the size of the dog, but there will be a great deal of growing to do in the weeks and months ahead, so do not let this worry you unduly.

Obviously, if you are intending to buy a puppy for the show-ring, you will have to go into the puppy's finer points in much more detail. Always bear in mind that the older the puppy, the more likely you are to be able to evaluate how the adult will eventually turn out. The puppy with probably the most potential will be solidly built, and fairly square when viewed in profile. This should mean that the back will be fairly short and the legs neither too long nor too short. When you look at the forelegs, they should not be too close together and should seem reasonably straight (without the toes obviously pointing outward in a 'ten to two' direction), though do bear in mind that the puppy will still have a lot of growing to do. There should not be a great gap between the puppy's elbow and the side of the body, and it is normal that the pastern will slope slightly. Looking at the puppy as it moves away from you, you will want the rear end to look nice and solid, the back legs not turning in, as in 'cow hocks', nor being too close together. Feet should be of moderate size and the toes should be compact and firm. Tails vary and frequently do not curl until the puppy is somewhat older, but the tail should be set correctly, which means that it must be high and it should be thick at the base.

Yacanto Fruitcake at Konishiki, pictured at four months old.

Photo courtesy: Linda Rupniak.

Taiyattangs David Bailey, pictured at four months old, showing lovely type with good bone. His coat colour is clear and the pigment is dark.

Photo: Bill Lilley.

The wrinkles on this five-month-old puppy will get less as he grows older.

Photo: Bill Lilley.

The head is likely to look somewhat large if the puppy is still young but, none the less, it should not appear to be out of balance with the body. You will be looking for nice small ears, pointing towards the eyes, and you must be satisfied that the eyes are free from defects. Although they are small and dark, they should not be so very sunken that you cannot see them. The bulge of the muzzle is more prominent on a puppy than on an adult and both the lips and the top of the muzzle should be well padded, but not overly so. The wrinkle will be more prominent on the forehead and cheeks, but you must be on your guard that there is not too much wrinkle. Be sure, too, that the lips can be rolled back easily to reveal the teeth and gums, but do bear in mind that the puppy may be at the teething stage, and so will not want his mouth interfered with too much. It would be wise to ask the breeder to show you the bite. The colour of the tongue is also important (see chapter 5) and the breeder should, therefore, also show you the tongue, as well as the roof of the mouth, so that you can check pigment.

The coat of the puppy should feel harsh to the touch. In a horse coat, the hair will be short, lying close to the body; whilst in a brush coat it will be slightly longer, though be on your guard against a coat which is too long. Because of the wrinkling in the shoulder region, the hair may appear longer here and may stand off from the body. This is quite normal. Regarding colour, this will possibly change with maturity, but the breeder should be able to advise you as to what the likely outcome will be.

PAPERWORK

When you purchase your new puppy, it is essential to receive a receipt from the breeder, especially if you have paid in cash. Please also bear in mind that, if you are paying by cheque, it is likely that the breeder will not allow you to take the puppy home until the cheque has cleared through the bank. This is only sensible on the part of the breeder, so do be prepared.

It will also be necessary to check that registration papers are in order. Hopefully they will already have arrived from the country's relevant Kennel Club but, should they not have done so, do make sure that you receive written confirmation from the breeder that the papers have been applied for, and discover whether or not any restrictions apply. In the UK, some breeders endorse pedigrees, stating that the dog may not be shown and/or bred from. This may be something which is to be in force for the rest of the dog's life, or it may be that an agreement is reached whereby the breeder agrees to assess the puppy when older and, if warranted, to lift the endorsement.

Other agreements, which can be entered into, are known as 'breeder's terms'. This means coming to an arrangement whereby the bitch one purchases is obliged, by the breeder, to have one or more litters – often by a stipulated age – and that certain puppies, usually the best, have to be given back to the breeder of the original bitch. Stud terms are another, less frequent, contract into which you might be asked to enter, involving the use of your male dog, at stud, on certain bitches of the breeder's choosing. *The permutations are virtually endless, and I would urge you to exercise extreme care before agreeing to any such arrangement.* In so many cases the best laid plans go wrong or, worse still, turn sour, so it is imperative that everything is laid down, explicitly, in writing, formally if possible. *If you just want a pet bitch and you have no desire to breed, do not allow yourself to be talked into a breeding programme.*

It is essential that the breeder tells you whether or not the puppy is, indeed, Kennel Club Registered (even if the papers are still awaited) and that a full pedigree is issued at the time of purchase. Just the name of sire, dam and grand-parents is not enough – a four or even five generation pedigree should be issued to you; this you will be able to refer to in the years to come and it will be an essential tool if ever you breed from your Shar Pei. If you are not already familiar with Shar Pei, the pedigree may not be as interesting as it would be if you knew some of the

This attractive five-month-old litter of puppies is evenly balanced in growth and development.

Photo: Bill Lilley.

ancestors behind your puppy, but a good breeder should always be willing to explain it and to tell you as much as possible about the dogs to which your own puppy is related, possibly also showing you pictures.

COLLECTING YOUR PUPPY

Your puppy's breeder should definitely provide you with a feeding chart so that you know the puppy's feeding routine to date. This you will be able to change in time, but it will be sensible to stick to the same routine, for a few days at least. You will, therefore, have to take the breeder's advice as to which make of food is given in those early days and, if the breeder uses a type of feed which is not easily available in general shops, you should ask if you can take a little home with you so that you can change the diet gradually. Some breeders will give you this as a matter of course but, if not, you should offer to pay for it.

Also be sure that the breeder explains the worming programme so that it can be continued as necessary. Personally I always give worming tablets with my puppies and strict instructions as to when they should be given and in what quantity. If your puppy's breeder does not do this, your vet will be able to advise you. However, the puppy should have been wormed routinely up to the date of departure and you should be told exactly when the last tablet was given. Likewise, you must know whether or not a vaccination programme has been commenced and, if so, an official vet's certificate must be given to you. Some breeders will ask for the cost of the vaccination to be paid in addition to the purchase fee, but this should have been agreed on the telephone beforehand.

When you collect your new puppy it is always best to have a family member or companion travelling with you, for the youngster is unlikely ever to have been in a car before and will need reassurance. In my experience, I find it best for all concerned if the puppy can be allowed to sit on the back seat of a car with an adult or a sensible teenage child. Cover the seat and have plenty of kitchen towelling at hand in case the puppy is sick on this first journey. Remember that, unless the course of vaccinations has been completed, which is unlikely, your puppy must not be allowed on to the ground to go to the toilet on the way home.

At this stage the puppy may or may not be used to a collar, depending upon whether or not the breeder has started to lead train. If a collar has been used, it is wise to put one on for the journey, but if not, do not upset the puppy with this now – there will be plenty of time when you reach home. Exercise extreme caution when getting in and out of the car so that your puppy does not jump out by mistake. Also, be careful that, during the journey, there can be no escape through an open window, should the puppy panic for any reason. Puppies frequently move more quickly than you expect!

ARRIVING HOME

Whilst I appreciate that you and your family will be tempted to play with the new puppy as soon as you get home, you must bear in mind that moving to a new environment is a big upheaval in any puppy's young life, and the car journey alone will have been tiring. Hopefully you will have sleeping quarters prepared so, after giving your puppy an opportunity for relief in an enclosed area of your garden on which no stray animals might have wandered, I suggest that you let your Shar Pei puppy take things quietly. Whilst some puppies do, indeed, strut around their new home as if they had spent their entire lives there, others are not so adventurous and will take time to adjust. At this early stage, don't over-fuss; let the puppy wander around in whatever area you have designated, so that part of the house becomes familiar, before extending the exploration. Friends and neighbours may be anxious to see your new, rather curious, arrival, but you will have to be firmly polite and suggest that they visit again when the puppy has settled in properly. The first night or so should be just for the puppy and your family.

I always suggest that, when people collect a new puppy, the timing is arranged so that the youngster does not arrive home too late at night. The late afternoon is always a good time for, after a little drink, perhaps something to eat and a good rest, the puppy will still have a couple of hours or so left to adjust to the new surroundings before the family turns in for the night.

MEETING THE FAMILY

The breeder will probably have shown you how best to hold the puppy but, if this is not the case, always remember that a puppy must never be picked up by just the paws or legs, nor by the scruff of the neck. One hand should be across the chest – being careful not to push the elbows out – and the other should be under the hindquarters, to give support. It is important that all family members know these rules and that, if children are subsequently allowed to play with the puppy, they are carefully supervised and not allowed to harm the puppy in any way, either by incorrect handling, or by being too rough.

If you have other pets in the household, again you should exercise care during the initial stages of introduction. A cat will, most probably, keep a good distance away at first, but will usually come around in good time and, before you know it, the two may have struck up a firm friendship. However, you must take care that the cat does not claw at the puppy's eyes. A small scratch on the skin will heal, but a scratch on the eye can lead to permanent damage, so do take care. My cat has a firm favourite in one of my own dogs and, whilst they love each other dearly, they will run around the house together like wild-fire and games can get too rough. Should this be the case in your household, see to it that the animals are never left alone together without supervision.

By all means let your Shar Pei puppy meet any other dogs in your household as soon as possible, but take things gently. Do not leave them alone together until you are completely satisfied that any older dogs will not harm the new puppy. Most mature dogs take well to new youngsters, but you must be sure that those who have been resident in your home longer than the newcomer are never allowed to feel as if they have been pushed out as a result. Lavish that little extra attention on them and they will adapt to the newcomer all the more readily.

Chapter Seven

TRAINING YOUR PUPPY

A Shar Pei puppy, like many other breeds, can be head-strong. As soon as a feeling of security in the home environment sets in, your puppy may well start to try to take advantage of the circumstances.This is very common and it is important that, right from the outset, you make it clear who is boss – you.

You must bear in mind that, in the early days and weeks of life in your home, the puppy will not know what is expected and so you will have to act as teacher, not too strictly, but with reassuring firmness. This attitude will pay dividends in the future, for it will teach your puppy respect for those in charge.

SLEEPING QUARTERS
You must provide proper sleeping quarters, somewhere to which the puppy is able to retire, freely and easily, when overtaken by tiredness. Although one always conjures up pictures of playful puppies in one's mind, in fact they sleep a great deal. At night time the puppy must be shown to the designated place and must be taught to remain there, even though, for the first few nights, your sleep is likely to be disturbed. If you take pity and allow the puppy into your bedroom at this stage, it will be virtually impossible to break the habit when the puppy is older.

The bed should be in an area away from draughts; if the base is about two inches from the ground this will help. Do not choose a wicker basket for, although they look pretty, puppies chew through them in no time at all, leaving sharp ends on which they may catch themselves. Those beds made of good strong plastic, which can be scrubbed out or hosed down, are the ones I find best. There is still a possibility that a teething puppy might chew the corners, making them rough, but such beds are quite inexpensive, so can be replaced without too much additional cost.

Whilst puppy is still small, the bed can be made to seem smaller and more snug by using plenty of veterinary bedding; and a clock, ticking in the room, will probably help your puppy to get off to sleep, should you find this a problem in the early days. Something which is very important is that the box is big enough to enable the puppy to stretch out at full length and yet not so large that the puppy can make a mess at one end and still settle down comfortably at the other. That will make house-training all the more difficult!

Some people like to use a thick cardboard box until the puppy has grown up a bit but I, personally, do not advocate this. Those who do choose such a box should be certain that it is not one which has been used for storing fruit or vegetables, in case any trace of pesticides used on the food remains on the box. Such a box must also be raised from the floor, to prevent draughts, and its base must be thickly lined with layers of newspaper under the veterinary bedding.

Soon enough your puppy will know where to sleep and, at the same time, you will have

If you start off on the right footing, your puppy will soon be happily established as a member of the family.

Photo: Bill Lilley.

embarked on house-training. If you buy a crate (indoor kennel) you will find that this is ideal for accomplishing both.

HOUSE-TRAINING

Shar Pei are instinctively clean dogs, which is of great assistance to the owner of a new puppy. Having said that, it is imperative that you help your puppy, from the very outset, to know where business can be done, and where not – though young puppies are not necessarily able to exercise control for long enough to tell you of the desire to go out if your attention is not caught immediately.

This means that, in the early weeks, you will need, as far as you can, to anticipate your puppy's needs. If you let the puppy out on wakening, immediately following a meal and again before bedding down for the night, this will enable relief to be obtained almost as frequently as needed. Also, following any vigorous play, it is wise to provide the opportunity to go outside, always remembering that the area must be one which is not used by stray animals until the course of vaccinations is complete and the vet has said that the puppy is free to go out wherever you wish to go.

Training in the use of a newspaper also pays dividends, for you are unlikely to have your eyes on the puppy for twenty-four hours a day, and there will be short periods when you will leave the puppy alone to avoid over-dependence on you. If a good thick amount of newspaper is placed near to the door, puppy can be directed to this when urgent need arises. The newspaper, and the door itself, will soon become associated as the place to go when relief is required. The very first accident can be used to your advantage. Moisten a small piece of newspaper in the urine and place

Puppies have to get used to lots of new experiences. This sixteen-week-old Shar Pei is exploring snow for the first time.

Photo: Bill Lilley.

this on the clean paper by the door. This should serve to act as a scent marker for future eliminations. Obviously, other than this initial training piece, any paper when soiled must be immediately removed and disposed of, the newspaper being replaced immediately by a fresh piece.

LEAD TRAINING

Even before being old enough to go out properly, your puppy should be familiar with the fact that a collar and lead will be used from time to time. Start by getting puppy used to just a collar, a lightweight one, which should be attached only for a moment or two at the beginning, gradually building up to longer periods as it becomes more acceptable. It is only natural that the puppy will scratch away at the collar on the first few occasions, so make sure that this exercise is supervised at all times so that no damage occurs.

When the collar has been accepted, you will be able to attach a lead. Different people have different methods of going about this part of the training. I like the puppy to walk around dragging the lead to start with, to get used to the fact that there is something attached to the collar. Clearly you have to be there all the time to see that the lead does not get inadvertently attached to anything or trips the puppy up while exploring. I then lightly take the end of the lead, and follow the puppy with it, so that the fact that there is a human on the other end is something that is hardly realised. Slowly you will be able to exert a little pressure on the lead, to which the puppy will almost certainly object at first. Remember to give plenty of praise when the puppy starts to walk in the general direction you are planning to go and, soon enough, you will have a proud puppy walking by your side. Never scold severely for the puppy not walking as you wish. Just be firm. Some puppies take to leads like ducks to water, but others need time to adjust to the restraint and require patience.

Whether or not you use tit-bits as a reward is very much a matter of preference. I know a lot of people who do train this way, but it is not a method which I favour. I have tried it, and though it seems, initially, to have the desired effect, in my experience the puppy comes to think that everything will be rewarded by a treat. Personally I prefer to reward just with kindness, something which is always available, doesn't put on weight and costs nothing.

As your Shar Pei will grow quite rapidly over the coming months, you will need to replace the lead you use for a small puppy with something stronger as maturity is reached. It would be a good idea to ask the breeder to show you what collars and leads she uses, if you are at all unsure. Obviously, if you plan to show, your Shar Pei will have to get used to a show lead, something we shall come to in a later chapter.

HOUSE RULES
Decide from the very outset whether your Shar Pei is to be allowed on the furniture or not. Should you allow free access to the furniture at the beginning, it will be taken for granted that this permission has been given for life – and bear in mind that your Shar Pei will grow as time progresses. If you do give freedom of the furniture, don't allow your puppy, when still small, to jump off anything. Always carefully lift your puppy down. Jumping off can do damage to the bones as they are forming and this is certainly not recommended for a dog destined for the show-ring. Should you not wish your canine companion to go on furniture, it will be necessary to correct any such tendency from the very start. A firm 'No' will be all that is needed, provided that you make this a rule from the outset. We must all bear in mind that dogs reason things out in different ways from humans and, if allowed to do something once, a Shar Pei will simply not understand why it is suddenly not allowed, so the motto is – start as you mean to go on.

FEEDING ROUTINES
As mentioned previously, your puppy's breeder should have issued you with a feeding plan telling you with what frequency your Shar Pei has been fed thus far, and with what food. It may be four meals a day, or perhaps this has already been cut down to three. Many puppies, on four meals, cut themselves down to just three, so your puppy will probably indicate when the time comes to have only three meals and, in time, only two.

In the first few days you should stick as closely as possible to the feeding plan which your puppy has followed with the breeder. A change of environment, and of people, will be quite enough for the puppy to cope with at the beginning, without also having to change diet and routine.

There are now so many excellent proprietary dog foods on the market that I shall not attempt to give suggested menus, though it appears to be frequent opinion within the breed that 'natural' foods are favoured above others, at least for the adult Shar Pei, so you may in time wish to look into these. When you decide to alter the diet, do so slowly. Never introduce a new diet and completely abandon the old one, as that will almost certainly lead to an upset stomach and, if you are not careful, you will also undo all the good work which has been done in house-training your puppy, as the chances of being 'caught short' will be greatly increased. Instead, put a little of the new food in with the usual meal and, gradually, add more and more so that, within a few days, the diet will have changed almost imperceptibly, and the puppy's stomach will have adjusted without any problem.

The Shar Pei grows quite rapidly and you will have to increase food intake accordingly. As the puppy matures, fewer meals will be needed, reducing from four to three and then to two. Some owners feed only one meal by adulthood but, in this case, it is wise to give a snack of some sort at the other end of the day. If you have a Shar Pei which gulps the food, feed several small meals rather than one or two large ones. Because of eating so quickly, the stomach may not be able to cope with the sudden intake, and the food will be vomited as a result. Added to this, by eating too quickly, too much air will be taken in with the food and this is said to encourage the onset of 'bloat', a life-threatening condition involving swelling of the stomach.

CHEWING

Your young puppy, while developing the full set of second teeth, will probably want to chew on virtually anything available. Although a Shar Pei's teeth will be through between the age of four and seven months, the teething process will continue until about a year old, as the teeth and jaw bones develop further.

Your Shar Pei puppy must be taught what is, and what is not, in order. The teeth can be sharp, so you must discourage any chewing of hands, in play, as well as chair legs, shoes and anything else which happens to look attractive, such as electric cables, which can be fatal. You will have to use a firm 'No' command, but you will also need to divert the pup's attention to something else on which chewing is permitted in order to ease any discomfort. There are many dog-chews available in pet stores nowadays and I am sure you will find something your puppy likes sufficiently well. Cows' hooves are much loved by dogs, but there is a risk that they may splinter, not to mention the fact that they can smell badly when well chewed. Pigs' ears, though not a very pleasant thought, seem much safer and equally enjoyable to a canine palate, though I do find that some dogs eat them rather too quickly for safety's sake, so if your dog gulps these, they ought to be avoided. The assorted hide chews, which can be bought virtually anywhere, are always a useful alternative – even though there are writers who have said that they can be dangerous, because the rawhide chunks mix with the saliva and can swell in the throat, if lodged there. I would not wish to dispute this but, in my many years in dogs, I have not encountered such problems. I find that my own dogs do not seem to like manufactured nylon bones, but these seem to be well thought of by many, especially in the USA.

Whether or not one gives a puppy bones is very much a matter of personal choice. The only

Konishiki Fatal Attraction JW, pictured at thirteen weeks. It is important to provide suitable toys to help your puppy through the chewing stage.

Photo courtesy: Linda Rupniak.

Early training will help your Shar Pei to become a well-socialised individual, getting on well with both people and other animals.

Photo: Bill Lilley.

bones I allow are marrow bones, and then only under close supervision. Other types of bone can certainly be dangerous, for they have a tendency to splinter and small pieces of bone can become lodged in the intestine, with consequent problems.

Giving your puppy something to chew will also help to keep the teeth reasonably free from tartar, a factor to which you will need to pay careful attention in adulthood.

If you find that your puppy, when confident about travelling and cured of any travel-sickness which may have been present at first, is inclined to chew inside the car, you would probably be wise to use a travel crate, rather than allow the freedom of a seat.

ANTI-SOCIAL BEAHAVIOUR

A growing Shar Pei puppy will undergo various hormonal changes and, especially if male, will very probably go through a spell of wanting to mount whatever is available, such as your leg or, worse still, that of a visitor to the house! This must be firmly discouraged and, as bitches can sometimes do it too, they also need to be told that this is not something of which you approve. Those owners who make a joke of it, and encourage their Shar Pei to mount legs in this way, are asking for trouble later on, when fifty or sixty pounds of dog is already in a habit which can be difficult to break.

AGGRESSION

When your puppy lived with the litter mates, a pecking order would have been established. Hopefully, the breeder will have made every effort to curb a puppy which took things too far, especially if any form of bad behaviour was expressed against humans.

If you see any sign of bad, or aggressive, behaviour in your own puppy, this must be curbed immediately. Things to look out for are barking, growling, guarding of objects, biting, snapping or general bullying. Such behaviour will get worse as the puppy becomes larger and older; it is not something which is "grown out of", however much you might wish this to happen. It is wise, always, to keep a strong collar on a Shar Pei with an aggressive instinct, so that control can be exercised easily. In reprimanding, take the dog firmly by the jowls, look into the eye and say, sternly, "No." Take care that the Shar Pei is held sufficiently firmly so that no injury can be caused to you, and there is no possibilty of a wriggle resulting in freedom. When things have calmed down, and only then, release your hold and put your dog down gently, giving praise for the eventual good behaviour.

It can also be especially beneficial, in the case of aggressive puppies, to train them to lie over on their backs to have their tummies tickled, something they enjoy but also something which helps you to become the more dominant party.

A Shar Pei which has a difficult temperament should always be given plenty of daily exercise for, if the mind is absorbed by other things, this will help to gear thoughts away from aggression. Don't give an aggressive dog too much attention, and only give praise during play, and when good behaviour has been clearly demonstrated.

It is most important that you never make excuses for your Shar Pei's bad temperament. You will only succeed in fooling yourself. Recognise the problem and take every possible step to correct it before it gets out of hand.

THE SHY PUPPY

Shyness in a puppy may be something in the breeding but it can also be caused, simply, by lack of socialisation. It may also be a combination of the two. A shy puppy should be exposed to new experiences; you should not give in to such a tendency and over-protect the dog. Ignore any protests and, gently, encourage the puppy to join in with activities.

A little obedience training can be of help for, if the puppy learns to walk at heel, there can be no hiding behind your legs. If Sit and Stay can be taught, this may, in time, make it possible for strangers to go up to make a fuss of the dog. If your Shar Pei allows this and stays as asked, you can give plenty of praise and this will help to build confidence.

A shy dog should be taken out frequently, so as to encounter new experiences, but it can take a long time to get a dog over this problem, so you will have to be very patient indeed.

CRATE TRAINING

I have already mentioned that a crate can be useful when transporting a puppy in a car and many owners of Shar Pei like their dogs not only to use a crate in the car but also at home. Certainly it can be useful to be able to confine a dog to a crate, for short periods, and many dogs really do treat them just like their own little home.

Your puppy will adapt more easily to a crate if introduced at a fairly young age. Put it in the sitting-room, or some other area of your house where there is plenty of activity and where the puppy, though crated, will not feel cut off from the activity of the household. A treat should be given to the puppy when this piece of furniture is first introduced, so that the association is with something good. To begin with, do not leave the puppy alone in the room at all, then, slowly, leave the room just for a moment or two. You will soon find that you can build up the periods of time during which you are out of sight, whilst your Shar Pei remains quiet. Never leave any dog in a crate for too long: in the early training stages, fifteen minutes or half an hour is quite sufficient.

If you have dealt with any problems which have arisen in your puppy's behaviour in a sensible manner, you should end up with a well-behaved adult Shar Pei which will do the breed proud.

Chapter Eight

CARE OF THE ADULT

Assuming that you have brought up your Shar Pei puppy with the care and attention needed during the formative months you will, hopefully, have a well-behaved, fit adult with which you can spend the coming years, be it a show dog or a pet. You will, though, be aware that, as the Shar Pei is not a dog living in the wild, you will still be depended on for many things in life. Adequate nutrition and exercise are two important aspects of your Shar Pei's adult life and you will, of course, have to spend some time keeping your dog's coat and body in good condition.

NUTRITION

First and foremost, it is essential not to allow your adult Shar Pei to become overweight, something which can happen and which will eventually put a strain on the heart, as well as on the joints. An overweight dog is at greater risk under anaesthesia and, perhaps surprisingly, appears to have less resistance to viral infections. Of course, your dog needs to be sufficiently well-covered, and so it is necessary to find that happy balance, feeding a sensible diet which is suited to the Shar Pei.

There are numerous highly nutritious, prepared dog foods available, so the choice is virtually without limit. Some dogs take to one brand, or selection of foods, in preference to others, but quality is important. Do not pump your Shar Pei too full of vitamins or additives, for they can unbalance an otherwise balanced diet. Many owners give one Vitamin C tablet per day, with the food, up to the age of about a year and then replace this with a teaspoon of cod-liver oil and malt in adulthood. It is thought that flaked maize, and maize oil, are not suitable for a Shar Pei.

If your Shar Pei carries too much weight when fed on proprietary dog foods, you should slightly cut back on the intake and substitute low-calorie food such as low-fat cottage cheese, green beans and other cooked vegetables. Shar Pei seem to enjoy boiled fish (watch the bones), tinned fish, chicken, turkey, rabbit, and lightly scrambled eggs as well as things such as rice pudding and cottage cheese. Tripe (not the bleached white tripe for human consumption) also seems to be a firm favourite with all dogs, but this does tend to put on weight, so, if your Shar Pei is subject to obesity, tripe should only be given as a treat. Plain brown boiled rice is also good for your dog and to this can be mixed any of the above favourites, with some vegetables. There are now complete foods made up of chicken and rice, or lamb and rice; Shar Pei owners have found these highly suitable diets. Grated raw vegetables can be given as an alternative to cooked ones and these are very nutritious.

Those dogs which get a lot of outdoor exercise need rather more food than those which lie around in the house all day and, in winter, those outdoors should have their daily food rations increased to help maintain body heat. It is also wise in winter to feed a little additional fat and to

CSPCA Ch. Thunder Moon's Sh-Boom (left) and CSPCA Ch. Thunder Moon's RSVP: A pair of well-cared for, well-trained adults – a credit to their owner/breeder, Colleen Kehe.

Photo courtesy: Colleen Kehe.

increase the foods which are higher in calories. Shar Pei, like all dogs, will accept the same food on a regular basis but I always feel it is wise to vary the diet, just slightly, from time to time. This also helps the bowel to adjust to change, so that if ever the diet does have to be changed due to travelling or lack of availability of the usual food, your Shar Pei's stomach should not become too upset. Any change of food, however, should be introduced gradually.

A supplement to the diet used by many Shar Pei owners is kelp, or seaweed powder. This is beneficial in many ways and can help to preserve good pigment, especially through the winter months. Use the recommended dosage for the size of dog.

PROBLEM EATERS
You may be unfortunate enough to have a Shar Pei which is a finicky eater; if so, give something to tempt the appetite. Popping a small, tasty piece of chicken in the mouth should stimulate the salivary glands and make your dog want more. Feeding twice a day is advisable and don't be tempted to give snacks between feeds, for you want your Shar Pei to be hungry when the food dish arrives.

Likewise, as I have mentioned before, a Shar Pei which gulps the food should be fed twice daily, or given several small meals, since, because of the speed at which the food is consumed, it may be vomited. Those which gulp also take in excess air with each mouthful and 'bloat', known also as gastric torsion, is a risk, so keep an eye on your dog during and after meals.

EXERCISE
Whilst you do not want your Shar Pei's shoulders to be overloaded with muscle, they should be firm when you feel them, rather than flabby. Another way in which you can check whether your Shar Pei is in trim is to take a careful look at the undercarriage. If it droops excessively, this is a sure sign that your dog needs more exercise than is currently being given – unless, of course, it is a bitch which has recently had a litter, in which case her body will take a little time to return to its former glory.

If your Shar Pei is kept in the house, you must give regular access to the garden for toilet

*Yacanto Fruitcake
at Konishiki:
Shar Pei enjoy the
challenge of
exploring new
surroundings.*

*Photo courtesy:
Linda Rupniak.*

purposes – always as soon as the dog wakes up and always immediately before bedding down at night, as well as at other intervals during the day. At least one controlled walk on a lead each day is also advisable, ideally alternating between a walk on a hard surface and on softer ground such as grass. Some Shar Pei enjoy swimming, so that is another form of exercise to which you may like to treat your dog, if you have a safe swimming area which you can use. Your Shar Pei will also get a fair amount of exercise in your own garden or run, and do bear in mind that, if you keep more than one dog together (not always easy with males), they will, to a certain extent, exercise each other in play and by chasing around. Teaching your dog to chase a suitably safe soft toy is also useful as a form of exercise, especially if your home is large enough to do this inside, should the weather ever be so bad that a walk is simply out of the question. When walking your dog on a road at night, you may wish to consider attaching a piece of reflective tape to the collar which can be seen easily by motorists.

COAT CARE
The Shar Pei's coat is fortunately one of those canine coats which tends not to give off a 'doggy' smell, even when wet. Its natural coarseness also has a tendency to repel dirt, which is an added bonus, and this is the case whether it is a horse- or brush-coated dog. Because the coat is short, it does not mat, and so constant brushing is unnecessary; just a light brush with a pure bristle brush – some prefer a grooming mitt – will keep the coat healthy, provided that your Shar Pei is being fed a balanced diet.

It is not necessary to bath your Shar Pei frequently, though lighter coloured ones can look fresher

Taiyattang Ivory Towers pictured at seven months old. A pale-coloured Shar Pei needs more attention to keep its coat clean, but you should not bath so frequently as to lose the natural oils in the coat.

Photo: Carol Ann Johnson.

at a show if they have had a bath beforehand. Some owners bath their show dogs as frequently as once a fortnight, but the majority bath only twice or four times a year, before each moult or before and after each moult.

This appears to be a good pattern for keeping the oils in the coat and yet free it from loose hair when necessary. How often you decide to bath your dog will, therefore, depend very much on your own dog's coat and colour. Dogs of a darker colour can usually be freshened up with a wet towel, though, of course, the occasional bath does not go amiss. One has to take care not to bath a Shar Pei too frequently as there is a risk of removing the coat's natural oil, which may lead to dryness and dandruff.

On those occasions when you do decide to bath your Shar Pei, it can be a good idea to plug the dog's ears with cotton wool to prevent water getting inside them – otherwise be extremely careful. I recommend that you use a mild human baby shampoo on the head, for this is less likely to irritate the eyes. Once this has been thoroughly rinsed off, you can work on the rest of the coat with a canine shampoo. Many Shar Pei owners say it is unwise to use a cream conditioner, because it softens the coat too much, whilst those who bath their dogs frequently advocate the use of a mild conditioner, which they feel helps retain the coat's natural oils. It must be stressed that the Shar Pei breed standard calls for a harsh coat.

Some owners say their Shar Pei dislike water and it is, therefore, wise to give the first bath at a fairly young age, so that your dog is accustomed to the procedure by the time maturity is reached. Obviously, a dog which has been bathed must be dried thoroughly before being allowed into the open air, so as to prevent a chill. Trimming of the Shar Pei's coat should not be necessary.

EARS

Because the ears are so small, it is imperative that they are checked on a weekly basis, so that any sign of infection can be picked up at the earliest opportunity. There are some extremely good, proprietary, ear-cleaning products available for sale at dog shows and in good pet shops. These make ear-cleaning easy, with the aid of a piece of cotton wool. Be sure not to delve too deeply into the ear canal, for this could cause serious damage. If there is any noticeable smell coming from the ear, your vet should be consulted and, provided no serious infection has set up, you will probably be asked to put in drops on a regular basis for a few days. Ear mites sound unpleasant, and indeed they are, but they are common in the Shar Pei and can be easily cleared up with something from your vet, provided that the problem is noticed sufficiently early.

Any scratching at the ear or shaking of the head is a clear signal that something is causing irritation, so check this as quickly as possible.

EYES

Especially when still teething, moulting or when a bitch is in season, there is a chance that your Shar Pei's eyes may blink or water slightly, something which can also happen if there is an ear infection or if the Shar Pei is stressed. Provided that entropion is not the cause, this will usually subside when the temporary problem has been solved. The face, and around the back of the ears, can be bathed with a mild solution of salt water and your vet should be consulted as to which eye-drops may be used if necessary. Always take care not to transfer infection from one eye to the other, so be sure to use a different piece of cotton wool to bathe each eye.

TEETH

I like to keep my own dogs' teeth clean throughout their lives so that, except in unavoidable circumstances, I do not have to subject a dog to an anaesthetic in order that a vet can clean them. There are various products now available to help with canine dental care, such as tooth-brushes and tooth-paste, and some large tablets which are to be chewed as an aid to removing plaque. Regarding the latter, I have found that my own dogs eat these so quickly that I cannot think they help a great deal, but perhaps for those dogs who chew them more slowly, they assist in keeping teeth clean.

It is of great help if your Shar Pei is given something on which to chew regularly, and I always feel that good, hard biscuits are as good as anything.

I use a professional tooth-scraper to remove any plaque which has built up, but this is something which you need to be trained to do by someone who has experience of using such a tool. It is of great assistance in keeping teeth free from plaque but it is sensible to train your youngster to accept such a scaler from an early age, even though you may only be 'going through the motions' for the first couple of years.

NAILS

To make the task of nail cutting simple, you should have already practised with your Shar Pei puppy when young. Nail cutting is much easier if you have a dog which will keep still and tolerate the procedure without wriggling about. The feet of the Shar Pei should be tight, and long nails will cause the feet to splay out, so it is imperative that nails are kept short. I find a 'guillotine' nail-cutter the most efficient. If you regularly exercise your Shar Pei on a hard surface, it is possible that the nails will be worn down naturally, but that is no excuse for not checking them from time to time.

A weekly check of nail length is necessary, and remember that the vein within the nail recedes only slightly each time the nail is cut. Some Shar Pei owners find it best to trim off a small sliver of nail about every four days and, in time, your dog will have nice short nails without you ever having caused any pain by having cut a vein.

Dark nails are more difficult to cut than light ones because the vein inside the nail cannot be seen. If you do catch a vein, this will be painful, and you will, once again, have to train your dog to be patient whilst nails are being cut if this has happened. I always keep potassium permanganate in stock in case of emergency; a little dabbed on will stem the bleeding very quickly. Although I have not tried it, I hear that ordinary household flour will have much the same effect on a bleeding nail.

HEAT AVOIDANCE
The Shar Pei is a hot-blooded dog and so it is unwise to allow any sitting for long periods in the sun, or close to a fire or radiator. This can cause the dog to scratch, and even to moult, earlier than would be expected. Sulphur tablets are a useful thing to keep in stock, for these can be given if the body overheats; usually about four tablets for six to eight days is the recommended dose. Under the arms and stomach you may also powder with 'Flowers of Sulphur', which will assist in cases of heat exposure.

BEDDING, KENNELS AND RUNS
Even if your Shar Pei lives in the house with you, a certain amount of time needs to be spent outside, especially in fine weather. Always keep in mind that draughts and dampness must be excluded at all costs, and there must be plenty of access to shade when the weather is hot. Any kennel, be it one just for daytime use or one in which the dog will sleep at night, must be raised from the ground slightly, so that air can circulate below, and so that water can run away freely when hosing down the run.

Be sure that the kennel is sufficiently large for your Shar Pei not to have to stoop to go through the door. If you are buying, or making, your kennel before your puppy is fully grown, do keep this in mind.

Dog runs can be made of many things but, having tried various types, I find that concrete ones, sloping away just slightly for drainage, with an additional area of 'Cotswold chippings', seem to work best. The concrete keeps the nails in trim, and the area of chippings (not too small or they will get caught in the pads) helps to keep the feet nice and tight. My own dogs also get the opportunity to run and exercise on grass, but I do not feel that grass is a suitable base for a dog run – in wet weather it can become a quagmire.

Whether or not you decide that your run should be covered is entirely up to you. It will depend partly on your family circumstances and how much time your Shar Pei will spend in the house. If you do have a covered run, be sure that air is able to circulate freely. I once sited mine too close to the garden fencing and found that it seemed to trap moisture, so that the run area was frequently somewhat damp. Not a success!

Wherever your Shar Pei is to spend time, there must be suitable bedding, and it is essential that this is thoroughly clean, especially if your Shar Pei is one with a tendency to suffer from sensitive skin. There are now a great many options open to you in this regard. Some people like shredded white paper, but I find that legs and feet tend to get caught up in this and prefer, in the kennel at least, a thick newspaper base (which must be changed daily) on top of which is a veterinary bedding. Any moisture is absorbed by the bedding and then the newspaper. Some Shar Pei owners find that man-made bedding causes their dogs to sweat, in which case you will need to use old cotton towels, sheets or bedspreads. However, these hold moisture, so they have to be checked very regularly and changed when necessary.

In the house, you must have a bed which is personal to your dog. Again remember that it should be away from draughts, so should be raised slightly from the floor. It is imperative that all bedding should be scrupulously clean, so that parasites find they have nowhere to harbour.

When using a disinfectant, it is always wise to check that it is not one which is likely to act as an irritant and, of course, nothing used should contain any poisonous element. Although your Shar Pei may not actually lick the surroundings, the dog's feet and pads, which can have been in contact with a surface that has been treated or cleaned with a potentially dangerous substance, will be licked.

CANINE INSURANCE

If you have only one dog, or a small number, it can be well worth taking out insurance and, in the case of Shar Pei, not an inexpensive breed, it could be to your advantage to take insurance out for all your dogs, even if you have several.

There are various forms of insurance offered by many different companies, so these you will have to investigate yourself. If you don't know where to start looking, begin with your vet's surgery. It may well be that he has leaflets available, or can point you in the right direction.

In general, the aim of canine insurance is to cover veterinary expenses, though the first few pounds usually have to be paid by you, and routine vaccinations are never included. Usually there are also restrictions on in-whelp bitches, so check this thoroughly before deciding which company to use. Another advantage of insurance is that, as well as cover for accidental death of the dog, there is usually an option on third-party cover, useful should your Shar Pei cause any damage.

VACCINATIONS

During adulthood, remember to keep a check so that your Shar Pei's vaccinations are adequately boosted, including those for parvovirus and for kennel cough. Vaccines change all the time, so you must take the advice of your vet in this regard, remembering that if ever you need to put your Shar Pei in a boarding kennel, you will need to show an up-to-date vaccination certificate.

Some owners prefer to use homoeopathy to help build up immunity against certain illnesses and, albeit not with a Shar Pei, I personally have experienced serious side-effects following vaccinations on one of my adult dogs, so I am always open to ideas about alternative methods.

There are certain vets who use entirely, or partially, homoeopathic medicines and I understand, from lectures I have attended, that some are convinced that the immunity provided by such means equals that of the more usual course of vaccinations. Unfortunately, in the UK, boarding establishments do not accept this form of prevention when deciding whether or not to accept dogs into their care.

PARASITE CONTROL

A clean environment will certainly help to keep your Shar Pei free from parasites, but even the cleanest dog can pick up something, like a flea, from time to time. There is no shame in this, so do not be afraid to consult your vet to see which method of control he recommends. Many new products have become available in recent years, and the canine press is a good place to find something to suit your needs. An interesting new product is now in tablet form. It is important that you follow the maker's instructions implicitly and always take especial care that no pesticide is allowed in the eyes, mouth or ears.

If you feel your Shar Pei's coat or skin is affected adversely by the use of parasitic sprays, powders or the new drops available, you may find that use of a mild anti-parasitic shampoo works sufficiently well.

Internal parasites can also be kept easily under control if you follow a regular worming programme. Do not be tempted to buy tablets from a pet store, but consult your vet as to the very best treatment available. A dog which does not have the unpleasant habit of eating sheep's droppings can usually be kept worm-free with tablets given routinely every six months. If you do exercise your dogs in sheep country, a more regular worming programme, including one for tape-worm, is advisable.

For those who prefer not to use the more usual veterinary tablets, homoeopathic treatments are available and I know that garlic is reputed to have the desired result.

CARE OF THE IN-SEASON BITCH

Whether or not you have males in your own household you must take especial care of a bitch in season, for males will go to any lengths to get to her and, if there are stray dogs in your neighbourhood, they may well present a particular problem, especially if they manage to find their way into your garden.

Do not, therefore, leave your bitch unattended outside and, when she is indoors, be sure that any males in your house cannot get in to her. Shar Pei are strong dogs and the difficulty of separating the two, once they have found each other, may just prove insurmountable, added to which a male which is aroused will not take kindly to being told to move off.

There are sprays and tablets which are supposed to eliminate the odour of a bitch in season. I am sure that they have a certain effect, but I doubt that any keeps males totally at bay. The odour may be unpleasant to the human olfactory organs, but if a dog wants a bitch he seems not to mind!

Because she leaves scent in her urine, try to wash down with a mild disinfectant whenever she relieves herself, as this will help the situation to some extent. It is unwise, as well as being unfair to others, to walk her in an area frequented by other dogs; so, if you do not have sufficient ground at home to exercise your bitch properly, she will have to be taken by car to a remote spot and exercised there on a lead. Always be aware of the strength of your Shar Pei bitch and, if you feel you could not cope at the approach of an unexpected male visitor, then don't take her – or make sure you are with someone sufficiently strong. Stay within sight of, and easy access to, the car, to which you can quickly retreat in an emergency. Personally, I would never exercise a dog in season on any public ground, but I know that people's circumstances vary and so the decision has to be yours.

Some people take their in-season bitches to dog shows, but I consider this unfair to the males, who are unlikely to be able to concentrate well on their performance in the show-ring if they have ladies on their minds.

Most bitches keep themselves fairly clean when in season but, unfortunately, a few do not, in which case you will have to check your bitch's back-end regularly. There is a canine sanitary towel available which can be of help if the bitch will accept it and use it sensibly. It will, of course, have to be removed to allow her to urinate. If you decide to try one, I hope you have more success than I have ever done!

I know that a veterinary surgeon can inject a bitch to keep her free from seasons, but this is something with which I strongly disagree. I know that things have improved as the years have gone by, but I strongly believe there is danger of such injections affecting her in an adverse way. It is said that, when the injections are stopped, she will again be able to conceive, but I know of several cases when owners have been unsuccessful in their attempts to get their bitch into whelp. I also know of many other cases when the temperament of the bitch has been upset by this alteration to her hormonal balance. If you are not prepared to cope with a bitch's seasons, then perhaps you should have had a dog or, alternatively, maybe you should consider having her spayed.

SPAYING

Before deciding that your bitch is to be spayed, please consider that this is a very final decision and she will never be able to produce a litter of puppies. After being spayed she is also likely to put on weight, so you will have to take care with her diet and be sure she is able to get plenty of exercise.

In any event a bitch should never be spayed prior to her first season; this something which is occasionally even recommended by vets, but which should be strongly discouraged. If you show your Shar Pei it is always wise to check your country's current Kennel Club ruling about whether or not she may be shown after spaying.

FALSE PREGNANCIES

Some Shar Pei bitches suffer from false pregnancies and this is a frequent reason for an owner taking the decision to have a bitch spayed. In cases of false pregnancy, take away any toys of which your bitch has become overly fond, as these she will treat as puppies. Homoeopathic remedies can be of great help in preventing false pregnancies.

KEEPING A MALE SHAR PEI

The male Shar Pei is a strong dog and is likely to be territorial, especially if he has been used at stud. Whether kept in the house, or in a kennel, it is essential that he is kept secure at all times for, if he were to escape and chase a cat or small dog, he could do untold damage. Most owners of Shar Pei males do not keep more than one male together, though they will usually live in perfect harmony with bitches.

In many cases, when a dog has been used at stud, he will be less clean in the house because he likes to mark his territory, and he is likely to become more dominant when in the company of other dogs.

CASTRATION

Castration of a male dog is sometimes a sensible course of action in the case of a pet which is not to be used at stud, or in an endeavour to calm aggressive temperament. The latter seems frequently to achieve some measure of success, but not always. Again, if your plan is to show your dog, check the current Kennel Club ruling about this.

SENSIBLE AND POLITE OWNERSHIP

There is a strong anti-dog brigade and so it is wise not to give them anything to complain about. There are laws relating to dogs, so one should always see that these laws are abided by. All dogs should have some means of identification, so that if they are lost, or stolen, their owner can be contacted, and of course no dog should ever be allowed out of the house to roam alone.

Teach your Shar Pei to defaecate only where it is permissible, and always clear up afterwards. There are special gadgets available for this purpose, but a strong polythene bag will do just as well, and is easy to carry in your pocket wherever you go.

The English Kennel Club now operates a Good Citizen Dog Scheme; if you wish to be sure that the behaviour and basic obedience of your Shar Pei is up to the standard required by this scheme, the Kennel Club can provide you with details.

Chapter Nine

SHOWING YOUR SHAR PEI

EARLY TRAINING

If you have purchased a Shar Pei with the intention of showing, you will need to give some training in your own home, beginning as soon as the puppy has settled in comfortably and has begun to feel secure in the new environment. Practise getting your puppy to stand still, as this is necessary in the show ring and, when you are sufficiently confident, get your family and trusted friends to go over the puppy briefly, just as a judge would do. At this stage, the mouth will probably be tender while the second set of teeth are coming through properly, so do not simulate a judge looking into the mouth and at the bite too soon.

Assuming that you have, by now, managed to get your puppy used to the lead, practise walking up and down, as if you were doing this for a judge. Get someone to watch you, so that you can take advice as to which pace suits your Shar Pei best. Every dog is set off to advantage by being moved, by the handler, at the correct speed, the one which highlights the dog's best points. When your Shar Pei moves confidently on your lefthand side (the most usual side for movement in the show ring), try to teach equally good movement on your right, for there may be times when this is required of you. However, do not rush into this; be sure you and your dog are sufficiently happy with movement on the left to start with – the last thing you want to do is to confuse your puppy at too early a stage.

SHOW TRAINING CLASSES

When your Shar Pei is fully covered by the vaccination programme you can, if you wish, go together to show training (ringcraft) classes; this can be a good way of socializing your youngster with other dogs and with humans too. I feel, however, that I must stress that you should be highly selective about the ringcraft class you choose for, though many are extremely good, there are some which are not. Your aim, at this stage of the game, is to learn as much as possible about the art of showmanship and, to do so, you will need to be guided by those who already have a great deal of experience. Not all breeds are shown in the same way and so the trainer should be familiar with the way a dog of similar size and substance is shown, even if he or she is not a Shar Pei owner.

In the UK the Shar Pei is a numerically small breed so you will, most probably, have to take the advice of experienced people in other breeds as to which ringcraft class might be the most suitable for you and your dog. Unless you live in the depths of the countryside, as I do, you will usually find that there is a good one within easy travelling distance of your home. If you have any difficulty locating one, your local vet may be able to point you in the right direction, or the Kennel Club keeps a list of approved ringcraft societies.

I would suggest that, on the first occasion, you go along without your dog, just to see what is

Thunder Moon's Bubbles Double (Am. Ch. Meiting Luv Wun MacMurfee – CSPCA Ch. Thunder Moon's Glad All Over): This pup is only eight weeks old and is already learning to stand correctly.

Photo courtesy: Colleen Kehe.

Yoshia Hooray Hallelujah at Konishiki, pictured at ten weeks. This dog went on to become Top Shar Pei Puppy in 1991 and Best of Breed at Crufts, 1992.

Photo courtesy: Linda Rupniak.

going on and to be sure that you feel confident that those running the class are sufficiently competent. As an alternative, you may take your dog along just to watch, on the first night, in order to become accustomed to the medley of strange sounds and all the different dogs, of varying sizes, which make up the class. When you do reach the stage at which you want your Shar Pei to participate, be careful not to stand next to an obviously aggressive dog and, if there is a very small or excessively agile dog in close proximity, do take care that no damage is done!

The majority of Shar Pei exhibitors free-stand their dogs but, even so, you must be very conscious of standing with the dog's legs in the correct place. A dog standing badly will look incorrect to the judge's eye and so it is to your advantage to get this exactly right. Again, use someone in whom you have confidence to tell you what angle looks best and, if you can avail yourself of a sufficiently large mirror, you can practise in front of this.

When you finally get into the show ring it will, of course, be necessary for the mouth of your exhibit to be inspected by the judge, who will need to know what the bite and dentition are like, as well as the colour of the tongue. Some judges will open the dog's mouth themselves and others will ask that you show them what they need to see. With all due respect to judges, I regret I have

Your Shar Pei will have to learn to have its mouth examined so that the judge can assess the bite and the dentition.

Photo: Carol Ann Johnson.

The Shar Pei's distinctive tongue colour also has to be assessed.

Photo: Carol Ann Johnson.

noticed several who seem not to be sufficiently familiar with the breed when judging and, consequently, fumble in the mouth; sometimes I doubt that they even see what they are looking for; and this cannot be good for an exhibit, which may be put off for future occasions. You must be aware that even very experienced judges in other breeds have often not had a great deal of opportunity to go over Shar Pei, simply because there are not many at shows, at least not at Open shows where up-coming all-rounders do their basic groundwork. If you feel that the judge is likely to disturb your exhibit by looking in the mouth, say quickly that you would like to show the bite and tongue yourself. This will be perfectly well accepted but, of course, you must know how to show well enough so that the judge can see everything necessary.

Your Shar Pei will grow and develop in many ways, and you are almost certain to find that the way in which you show your dog will need to change slightly as the months progress.

ENTERING SHOWS

Your Shar Pei, if correctly registered with the Kennel Club, will be eligible for entry at shows from the age of six months. This means that you will have to have started thinking about shows

LEFT: Linda Rupniak standing Am. Ch. Sheng Li Mon Ju Copious in the show ring.

Photo: Carol Ann Johnson.

BELOW: The judge 'goes over' a dog to assess conformation and soundness.

Photo: Carol Ann Johnson.

well in advance because, depending upon the type of show, entries can close several weeks beforehand. Exemption shows can be entered on the day, but these are really just for fun; the proceeds go to charity and there are never any specific breed classes on offer, just pedigree classes and novelty classes, such as for 'the dog with the waggiest tail'. Other shows, for which you must book in advance, include Sanction, Limited, Open and Championship Shows, and, if you plan to be a serious exhibitor, your concern will principally be with the last two. Only occasionally are there Shar Pei classes at Open Shows in the UK but, nonetheless, if you are completely new to showing, it would probably be wisest to begin with these, at least until you get to know what you are doing. Fees at Open shows are less expensive than at Championship events and the atmosphere is often more relaxed, though you may find that you have to enter an Any Variety class, rather than one specifically for Shar Pei. The number of Shar Pei exhibited in a breed class varies according to many factors, including the location and how highly the judge's opinion is likely to be valued.

Championship Shows are usually benched in the UK (meaning that benches are provided on which dogs wait between classes), although very few are in the US. Fees are charged for every dog entered, and for the number of classes entered, and so by the time you have added the extra cost of catalogue, travel and out-of-pocket expenses, you can see that the financial layout for serious showing amounts to quite a hefty sum, especially when campaigning more than one dog.

When you have obtained your show schedule from the society's Secretary, the details having been published in the canine press, consider carefully the classes you should enter. Do not make the mistake, which is done by so many novices, of entering every available class. The Open class, for instance, is open to all but can include top winning stock, providing an unfair test for your unfinished youngster. If your dog is really new to showing, I suggest you restrict entries to exhibitions in the most appropriate age class. The show schedule will include a list of qualifications which allow dogs entry to classes, and you will need to keep a careful record of your dog's wins so that you never, mistakenly, enter a class for which your Shar Pei is not eligible. Entries are pre-paid and so, if you own a bitch, there is always the chance that you enter a show and then she comes into season beforehand. There is no rule to say you cannot enter, but the owner of a bitch in full season is unlikely to be popular with exhibitors who have taken male dogs along to the show. The bitch may also be a bit skittish before and during her season, due to a change in hormone balance, and you may well decide that, all things considered, it is best to leave her at home and forego the entry fees.

TRAVEL ARRANGEMENTS

Always allow yourself plenty of time to travel to a show; you may need to stop to exercise your dog on the way and you could meet with unexpected traffic delays or long queues into the showground's car park. Nothing is more frustrating than travelling a long distance to a show, only to find that you have missed your class. Because it is not a numerically strong breed, Shar Pei frequently follow another breed into the ring, meaning that they are not judged at the beginning of the day. However, there is always the chance that things may change, or the breed scheduled before may be judged especially quickly, so it is in your best interest to arrive in good time for the start of the day's judging. It is a good idea to pack the car the night before and to fill up with petrol, in case you leave home before the garages are open; also check the canine press for notification of any change in judging times. If you wish to keep your costs down, you would be well-advised to take along a packed lunch and a flask of coffee, something which is essential if travelling in the depths of winter, when there is a risk of being stranded in the snow on the way to or from a show. Never, of course, forget to keep an ample supply of fresh water in the car for your dog.

STYLES OF HANDLING

ABOVE: Peter Clarkson showing his successful import Am. Ch. Panache Times a Wastin.

LEFT: The handler is keeping the attention of Konishiki Gipsy Dance at Kyushu by attracting with a tidbit, inside his trouser pocket.

Photos: Carol Ann Johnson.

ARRIVING AT THE SHOW

Hopefully you will arrive at the show in good time, so that you can sort out where your bench is situated in proximity to the ring. You will need a benching chain, so that your Shar Pei can be left on the bench without any means of escape. It is not always easy to find such chains in pet shops but you will, certainly, be able to buy one from a stall at the first major show you visit. Because the Shar Pei needs little grooming at the show, you will not need to take along a great deal of equipment, but do make sure that your dog is clean and that you have something with which to freshen up the face, should the need arise. As Shar Pei can suffer from sun-burn more easily than other dogs, you should always be aware of this and carry with you some means of protection against over-exposure.

RIGHT: Carole Lilley showing Ir. Ch.
Taiyattangs Smiffy
The Last Emperor.

BELOW: Some exhibitors feel they get
the best out of their dogs by standing
slightly in front.

Photos: Carol Ann Johnson.

New exhibitors will need a ring-clip, something which you can buy, in the UK, for about 25 pence at many stalls, unless you want a better quality one – perhaps depicting a Shar Pei's head. This will be required to keep your dog's ring number in place, for it must be visible at all times; if you arrive in the ring without your number, the steward will most probably send you away again to collect it, and you will certainly not be allowed to be judged until it is displayed. At benched shows ring numbers are usually found on the bench allocated to your exhibit, but they may be given out by the steward in the ring or, at smaller shows, may be obtained from the Secretary's office. Make sure you know the whereabouts of your number before you enter the ring, for you want to be able to concentrate a hundred per cent on your dog, and not be worrying about your number.

An important rule, for successful exhibitors, is to keep your eye on the judge at all times, and that means from the very moment you enter the ring with your dog. Even though the judge may be enjoying a cup of coffee between classes, you will notice that his or her eye may well wander along the line of dogs as they come into the class. Avoid standing next to someone who is renowned to be a chatterbox, for you will need to concentrate entirely on your exhibit, always keeping one eye on the judge so that you never miss an opportunity which may be given to you to move your dog again for further appraisal. Watch especially carefully when the judge is calling the winners into the centre of the ring for, if you do not go out when called, you may find that you are not given a second chance.

WINNING – AND LOSING

Finally, whether you win or lose, do it with good grace. There is always another show and another judge and, who knows, the placing might just be reversed next time around. It is usual, if your dog has been placed second or third, to congratulate the class winner and you must never, under any circumstances, refuse a prize card or rosette – that is the epitome of bad form and risks grave consequences if the judge chooses to report the misdemeanour to the Kennel Club. If you do not agree with a judge's final selection, that is your prerogative and you need not enter under that same judge again, but you would be wisest not to comment out loud.

If you are lucky enough to win your class, of course you will be delighted, but try not to be too boastful about it. In the dog-showing world there are those who boast excessively, and they are never the most popular people amongst the canine fraternity! A dog who has won a breed class, and has not been beaten in another class, will be eligible to compete for Best of Sex or Best of Breed, depending upon the classification at the show. Under no circumstances withdraw your dog from such competition (unless, for example, the dog has gone lame), for this is also considered the height of bad manners. Likewise, if your dog is eligible to compete for Best in Group, Best in Show or Best Puppy in Show, it is considered courteous to the judge, who gave your exhibit that opportunity, to enter the competition. If you are fortunate enough to have a major win, you should consider carefully whether to spend some money advertising this in the canine press, so as to bring it to the attention of others, including those who judge the breed. You will often find that there is a canine photographer at the show and so you will be able to have your dog's photograph taken.

Looking on the negative side, if your 'potential show dog' turns out not to be of a sufficiently high standard to achieve consistent success in the show ring, love the dog as a much-valued pet. After all, it is hardly the dog's fault for growing up to be not quite as typical of the breed as you had hoped, but you will have learned a great deal from your many experiences together.

Chapter Ten

BREEDING SHAR PEI

Before looking at the very serious subject of mating I feel it is, first of all, important to stress that the decision whether or not to mate your Shar Pei bitch has to be considered extremely carefully. *Let us do away, immediately, with the myth that 'one litter is good for a bitch'. This is pure fiction and many a bitch has led a happy, fulfilled life without ever having had a litter.*

POINTS TO CONSIDER

There are many essential points to be taken into account. *The bitch must be of good enough quality to breed from.* Look at her carefully and, if necessary, ask the opinion of someone more experienced than yourself. Is she really a sound, typical specimen of the breed? Does she have any hereditary defects which you would not like to produce in her offspring? Is her temperament

Spirits Incantation Thunder Moon (left) and Am. Ch. Thunder Moon's Chicago Fire with owner/breeder, Colleen Kehe. Breeders have a great responsibility for the future well-being of the breed.

Photo courtesy: Colleen Kehe.

ABOVE: Ir. Ch. Taiyattangs Silk Stockings (left) with her sire, Ir. Ch. Taiyattangs Smiffy The Last Emperor: Evidence of a well-planned breeding programme.

LEFT: Taiyattang Heaven On Earth: grand-daughter of Ir. Ch. Taiyattangs Smiffy The Last Emperor, pictured at four months.

Photos: Bill Lilley.

sufficiently sound that she is likely to make a good mother? Also, ask yourself why you wish to breed. One's aim in breeding should never be merely 'to produce a litter of puppies'. Anyone can do that and such an attitude will in no way benefit the breed as a whole. Personally, I only breed a litter when I need to keep one of the litter for myself, and that, I feel, is the correct attitude. Of course, there are 'commercial' breeders of all types of dogs, but I consider that no bitch should be used as a money-making machine.

Consider also that you must have sufficient time to spend with the bitch and her litter. It is simply not fair, on either the bitch or her puppies, to expect to hold down a full-time job. Even if you only work part-time, you will need to arrange for plenty of time off when the litter is born, including a few days before the due date, in case your bitch whelps early. You must also be financially stable, so that you can provide the bitch and puppies with all their needs and veterinary requirements. Breeding a first litter, especially, can be an expensive exercise – X-rays to check for hip dysplasia is just one of the preparations to be made.

CHOOSING A STUD DOG
Having said all that, let us assume that you have carefully considered your reasons for wishing to bring a new litter into the world and have decided this is the right thing to do. You will need to consider which would be the best possible stud dog to use on your bitch. You will have studied your bitch's pedigree carefully and found out as much as possible about her ancestors. If they are dogs which you have not seen yourself, ask those who have seen them, so that you gather together as much information as possible. In a breed as 'young' as the Shar Pei, bloodlines are still limited, so it is even more important that you do not introduce, into your own breeding line, faults which you would rather were not there. They will not be easy to breed out.

Look not only at the quality of the males which you are considering but, also, at the offspring they have produced. This is equally important, if not more so. When assessing the offspring, take into consideration the bitches to which they have been mated. Are any of these of similar breeding to your own Shar Pei bitch? If so, you will have a better idea of what your own bitch is likely to produce, though do bear in mind that every dog has a different genetic make-up.

BREEDING PROGRAMMES
So, one needs to look at both genotype (genetic make-up) and phenotype (outward appearance), and I would suggest you read a book specifically about breeding if you wish to go into this more deeply. You will also wish to consider whether you are in-breeding, line-breeding or out-crossing by using your chosen stud. In a breed such as the Shar Pei it is appreciated that, because in many countries blood lines are still limited, the choice may be restricted to a certain extent.

I would strongly suggest that new, or relatively inexperienced breeders, avoid inbreeding to start with. Inbreeding is a powerful tool but, though it is a way of stamping one's mark on one's bloodlines, it is something which can also have very negative consequences if one does not understand fully the breeding and genetic make-up in the dogs behind the selected partners. Again, this is not a book in which there is sufficient space to go into breeding in great depth, but in-breeding involves father-to-daughter, mother-to-son and litter-brother-to-sister matings. Some people also consider that half-brother to half-sister matings are in-breeding but, technically, this is on the border-line between in-breeding and line-breeding. I would not recommend it in the early stages of developing your breeding programme.

It is generally accepted that line-breeding is the most favoured method; that is to say, when the bitch and the dog have *at least one* common ancestor, usually in the first few generations of the pedigree. For example, grand-daughter to grandfather is a combination which many consider works well but, again, I must stress that this all depends on the genetic make-up of those involved.

Out-crossing is when there is no related blood in the first few generations; put in simple terms, when you look at normal five-generation pedigrees you can see no names behind the bitch which are the same as those behind the dog. Such a mating may be necessary if you are using a Shar Pei import but, again, my personal advice would be to line-breed for your first litter and then, when you have some idea of what your bitch has produced, perhaps consider out-crossing at a much later stage – and only then if you have sufficient knowledge of the bloodlines behind the out-cross. It is preferable that any out-cross which is used as sire is line-bred, for if he, too, is the result of an out-crossed mating, there will be so many new blood-lines mixed up in his pedigree that it will take you several generations of breeding before you can be reasonably sure what is actually there.

Something else it is important to bear in mind is that, if your bitch is to be mated for the first time, it would be better if the stud dog could be one who is experienced. A maiden bitch teamed up with a maiden dog does not always make for an easy mating and, after all, you may well have wanted to see what offspring the dog has already produced.

You will have gathered that the choice of sire should in no way be determined by the convenience factor. *Just the fact that a seemingly good dog lives within easy travelling distance does not make him the best sire for your bitch!* You will have to be prepared to travel to the stud dog and, if there are to be two matings, which is usually advisable, it is wise to leave a full day in between, so an over-night stay may be necessary. This is something which you will have to discuss with the owner of the stud. Some stud dog owners have facilities for keeping bitches for a few days, in which case an additional charge may be made, but others simply do not. You will need to discuss these arrangements, should it be that the stud dog you plan to use is not within reasonable travelling distance of your home. If you do leave your bitch with the stud dog owner for a day or two, take along some of your bitch's own bedding and, perhaps, a favourite toy, to help her settle down well in a strange environment.

You should see to it that your bitch is brought fully up-to-date with her vaccinations before she comes into season, so check with your vet as to whether or not boosters are due. She should also be wormed around this time, for bitches can pass worms to their puppies. It is better that she be wormed prior to her mating, so that the litter is less likely to suffer from internal parasites when young.

BOOKING THE STUD DOG
When you have decided on the best possible stud dog for your bitch, you should book the mating with the stud dog owner, ideally several months, or at least weeks, in advance. If you have followed my advice, you will already have seen a copy of the dog's pedigree, so it is likely that you have already made contact to obtain this. You will also have asked to see proof of his hip-score, if he has been tested for Hip Dysplasia (HD). Some dogs are at 'limited stud', meaning that their owners are highly selective about the bitches which are brought to them and matings are limited to a certain number per year. It is essential that adequate notice is given to the stud dog's owner. Many owners, quite rightly, do not like their males to be used too frequently and some insist on a certain interval between matings.

It is wise also to have a second choice of stud lined up, in case the best laid plans go wrong. It may be that the dog is simply not interested in the bitch or, alternatively, that she will have nothing to do with him, whereas she may be much more receptive to a different dog. It is only courteous to the owner of your second-choice dog to explain exactly what the situation is. Indeed it may be that your second choice is owned by the same person, for it could well be a close relative of the former, if you are aiming to bring in certain blood-lines.

STUD FEES AND TERMS

Prior to the mating you should also have discussed the matter of stud fees and have agreed when such fees are to be paid. Different people work on different terms but, in my opinion, it is best that the full fee is paid at the time of the first mating. Should no puppies be born as a result, it is usual that another mating, to the same dog, is offered at the bitch's next season, at no extra charge. Some people, however, ask for part-payment upon mating, and part when a live litter has been produced, but it should always be remembered that a stud fee is for the actual mating service and that, if no puppies are produced, that is not always the fault of the sire. Another arrangement which occurs is that one or more puppies are taken by the stud dog owner either in lieu of payment of a stud fee or as part payment. Whatever arrangements are made, it is essential that they are set down in writing, so that each partner in the contract knows what is expected. If a puppy is to be given to the stud owner, at what age will the choice be made? Who makes that choice? And is it to be first, second or third pick? The permutations are endless, so, to save any difficulties arising later, I stress again that any arrangements made must be in writing and both the owner of the stud dog and of the bitch should retain a copy, duly signed and dated.

Some owners of stud dogs insist that the bitches which are brought to their dogs have had a swab taken by their vet, providing proof that the bitch has no vaginal infection. This may be something you wish to have done in any event, to set your own mind at rest. Should there be infection present at the time of the mating, this can produce problems in the whelps, which may be malformed.

GETTING THE TIMING RIGHT

The main indicator as to whether or not your bitch is ready for mating is the size of her vulva. You should feel this, carefully, a few weeks before she comes into season and again when she is in season. By placing your thumb across the top, you will find that it suddenly goes much softer and more palpable, in addition to which it has become noticeably larger. It is now that she is ready. Her tail will also be held over to one side when you touch her rear end, though she may do this throughout her season. Bleeding may or may not have stopped when mating time arrives, so I do not think it wise to take this as a reliable guide. Certainly many bitches seem to have stopped bleeding when the time is right, but others do not. It is usual for the bitch to travel to the stud; this is certainly to be recommended and, indeed, is expected by the stud dog owner. A stud dog is far more likely to perform well on his own territory and there are certain stud dogs who have their own designated stud area, in which they apparently perform more readily.

If you have your own stud dog, and provided that he is genuinely the most suitable choice for your bitch, it may be that you are mating dogs in your own home and it is likely that the two will be familiar with each other. In some cases dogs which live together are reluctant when it comes to mating but, in most cases I have encountered, there have been no difficulties in this regard.

The bitch will be receptive to the male only for a few days, usually three, four or five, and these will be the days on which the stud dog is willing to take most interest. At other times during her season he may also be interested but will not mount or, if he does so, his attempts will be in vain. Every bitch's cycle is slightly different but, in many cases, she will be ready for mating somewhere between the tenth and sixteenth day. It is essential that you know exactly when her season started and that she is checked on a daily basis, for I have known of bitches ready as early as their fourth day and as late as their twenty-sixth.

THE MATING

When the time comes for your bitch to be mated, the owner of the stud dog will, hopefully, be someone who is experienced in such things and will tell you exactly what is expected of you.

The tie: This can vary in duration from a couple of minutes to forty-five minutes or longer. It is not essential in order to achieve a successful mating, but most breeders prefer a reasonable length of tie to take place.

Photo: Bill Lilley.

Many stud dog owners prefer the bitch's owner not to be present, so as not to distract her from the job in hand. Should this be the case, you are within your rights to ask for photographic proof that the mating has taken place with the dog you have booked. It may seem a strange request but, if you are not present and if no puppies result, or if the puppies are not as you expect, you may have doubts in your mind.

A tie will usually take place when the dog has penetrated the bitch, meaning that the two are locked together for a while, sometimes just for two or three minutes, sometimes for over an hour. About ten to twenty minutes is normal. It is important that fresh water is available for the dogs, though they are unlikely to bother about a drink whilst they are so involved!

A slip mating is when the dog penetrates the bitch and ejaculates (as far as one can tell) but no tie takes place, so he comes out of the bitch almost immediately. Such matings are not uncommon in the inexperienced stud and can most certainly produce puppies, though in the case of slipped matings I would always recommend a second mating about twenty-four hours later. Puppies can be conceived at each mating and therefore, although some owners have three matings, I like to restrict it to only two, provided I am confident that they have been satisfactory. For the same reason, I do not consider it wise to have too long a gap between matings, for there is the risk of some puppies being much further advanced than others, which can cause difficulties at the time of whelping.

Bear in mind that a bitch can conceive to more than one dog so, if she is mistakenly mated by two different dogs during her season, some puppies will be sired by one male and some by another – so take care!

If you are invited to be present at the mating, please be sensible about the seriousness of the situation. Do not take younger members of the family along for a lesson in the facts of life. Believe me, as a stud dog owner, I have had some peculiar visits from people and I feel it unfair on both the owners of the dog and the dog himself. Do not be over-possessive of your bitch; she may scream out briefly as the dog first penetrates, especially if it is her first experience, but this is not unusual and she will soon have plenty to take her mind off the initial discomfort!

You may be asked to assist with the mating, for it is important that neither the bitch, nor the dog, is allowed to pull away, risking damage to the male's penis, because the bitch's vulva will have contracted, preventing escape. Both dog and bitch should wear strong leather collars so that they can be held by these, if necessary. Even the best-tempered dog, or bitch, can turn around to snap if hurt at all. You must be on your guard for this, for the sake of all parties present. Some people prefer to muzzle their bitches, using a lady's stocking tied around the muzzle with a half knot and secured at the back of the neck. This will allow the bitch to breathe, and salivate, freely but she will not be able to open her jaws wide enough to bite.

When the mating is finished it is wise not to allow the bitch to pass water for a short while, so it is important that she has been given the opportunity to relieve herself before the mating took place.

When the mating is finished, I like the dog and bitch to spend at least a few more moments together, but it will be up to the stud dog's owner. This is the time when they will usually be calm in each other's company and it is an appropriate moment for the humans involved to settle up matters of paperwork and finance. Be sure to receive a receipt if you have paid a stud fee at this point.

In some countries Artificial Insemination, more commonly known as AI, is used; but this is currently accepted by the English Kennel Club only under very exceptional circumstances, and I leave it to other authors to cover this in depth.

THE PREGNANCY

The average gestation period for a bitch is sixty-three days but the puppies can quite easily be born a few days early, or late, and I have known healthy litters born even a week early.

Following the mating you will, understandably, be anxious to know whether or not your bitch is expecting a litter, but the early signs are difficult to detect. I usually find that the bitch's vulva does not shrink back quite to normal size following her season, if she is in whelp, and her nipples tend to be a little more pink, and firm, than usual. However, these signs are by no means certain and you will probably have to wait until she is five or even six weeks in whelp before you are sure. Of course, it is possible to have tests done by your vet; but I, personally, don't like to subject my in-whelp bitches to undue trauma and would rather let nature take its course, unless I am unduly worried about something. By about the fifth week you should be able to see signs of thickening around her middle and loss of her 'waist'. At this time, you should also begin to see a noticeable change in her nipples and you may see a clear discharge from her vulva, so you will need to keep this area clean and fresh. Should the discharge be coloured, you should visit your vet to get your bitch checked over.

The young puppies will develop very slowly during the first few weeks of pregnancy, so do not expect your bitch to require heaps more food from the word go. She will tell you when she needs more food. However, throughout her pregnancy, you should see that her food is of the highest quality, possibly increasing the protein intake, though not dramatically so. As her abdomen starts to fill up with the puppies, she should be given smaller, more frequent, meals as she will not be able to cope with one large meal and therefore may feel hungry a few hours later. There may be days when she feels a little off-colour and does not wish to eat much, so tempt her with a small portion of her favourite food, to stimulate her appetite. Not until she is within a day or two of producing the litter should you expect her to go off her food dramatically.

Supplement her diet with vitamins and minerals, though not to excess. This is something about which your vet, or an experienced Shar Pei breeder, will be able to advise you.

Throughout the period of pregnancy do not over-fuss her; she is not ill, just pregnant. If you make too much of a fuss of her, she may rely too heavily on you for help when the puppies are born. She will, gradually, reduce her periods of exercise but it is essential that she goes for a short,

The American import, Lindseys Sweet N Swingn Sami at Taiyattang, pictured eight and a half weeks in whelp. This bitch has a superb temperament. She also has tiny ears which are curled at the edges. These are much sought-after, but seldom seen.

Photo: Bill Lilley.

leisurely walk at least twice a day to keep up her muscle tone. She should not, however, be allowed to climb anything steep, nor to jump, as this could risk inducing early labour. In the week prior to her due date of whelping, she should always be supervised when out for exercise, just in case she is one of those bitches who might take you unawares and whelp early.

Many people use raspberry leaf tablets as an aid to whelping and, I have to admit, on the one occasion that I used them, my bitch had no whelping difficulties at all. The person who had the difficulties was me, for the bitch gave me no indication at all that she was ready to produce her litter (her first); just a little yell as the first puppy was about to pop out. I was taken entirely by surprise and of this I thought it prudent to warn you.

PREPARING FOR THE WHELPING

A couple of weeks or so before your bitch is due to whelp, you should prepare the whelping box and, though she will not wish to stay in it at this stage, it should be shown to the bitch so that she will be familiar with her surroundings at the time of whelping.

There are several first-rate, ready-made whelping boxes available for sale on stands at dog shows so I would suggest that, if you have not before whelped a litter, you should go along to have a look at these. Even though you may decide to make your own, rather than buy one, they will serve to give you ideas as to the best design.

It is important that, like the bitch's usual sleeping quarters, the whelping box is raised slightly from the ground to give protection against draughts, and it should be in a quiet place, away from unnecessary disturbance and other dogs. While being sufficiently big for your bitch to lie out in it at full stretch, the whelping box must not be so large that she cannot use the sides to push against, when actually producing her whelps. It will need removable guard rails inside. These are a few inches high and a few inches away from the sides, so that the puppies have some means of escape, should they get trapped between the back of the bitch and the side of the whelping box. They are an invaluable aid, for, however careful bitches might be, accidents are always likely to occur when a bitch is asleep or fully occupied with those puppies she can see. Usually a lost puppy will cry, but this may not be heard if the bitch is lying on the youngster. The rails will not be in place at the time of whelping but fitted in when whelping is complete. They can be removed again when the puppies are up on their feet and better able to fend for themselves.

The whelping box must be made of a substance which can be easily cleaned and I always like to have a front section which pulls down, so that I can comfortably have access to the front of the box when the bitch is actually giving birth. Some boxes have extendable sides, which can be built up higher as the puppies grow and become more active, but they must never be so high that the bitch is not able to get away from the puppies when she chooses to do so. I also have a detachable run area so that, when the puppies are up on their feet, they can have more area in which to play; this area can then be closed off again when they need to sleep.

You will need to provide heat in the box and some modern ones are fitted with heated pads. However, I prefer to erect an infra-red heat lamp above the box, positioned slightly off-centre. If this has a protective cage below the bulb, it is quite safe but, naturally, care must be taken that no wires are accessible to the bitch or her puppies. Such a means of heating allows the bitch to move away from it when she wishes to do so and yet she can still remain with her puppies, which can lie, if they choose, under the direct heat when not feeding. It is imperative that puppies have sufficient warmth, especially for the first two or three weeks of their lives.

In addition to the whelping box, you will need to have collected a large supply of clean newspaper with which to line the box. This will have to be changed frequently while the puppies are being born. The quantity you will get through will be quite unbelievable, so do make sure you stock up well. If possible, try to strike up a friendly relationship with your local newsagent, so that you can have those papers which are unsold and yet unused – an ideal situation. You will also require suitable bedding inside the box for when whelping is over and bitch and puppies need to settle down comfortably.

About a week before the litter is due, telephone your vet to advise him that your bitch is due to whelp. In the event of needing to call him out to your house outside surgery hours you, and he, will be glad that you have kept him informed, especially if the call-out is in the early hours of the morning.

At the time of whelping, you will also need a small cardboard box in which to put the new-born puppies whilst the next whelp is being delivered. This box should be lined with paper and a not-too-hot water bottle, covered in a towel, so that there is no fear of it burning the puppies. The puppies can be loosely covered over with a clean light-weight cotton towel whilst in the box: this should prevent them from crying and disturbing their dam.

It is also necessary to have a covered receptacle available for any puppies which are still-born. This should be kept well away from the whelping box but it is only sensible to have it available. As you will have an enormous amount of rubbish to tidy away during whelping, a good supply of black plastic bags is also a priority. Other items which you will need for the whelping are plenty of white kitchen towelling paper, clean cotton towels, soft gauze, water, if a supply is not available in the whelping room, a nail brush and surgical scrub, for it is essential, both during whelping and whilst the puppies are very young, that your hands are scrupulously clean. Kitchen scales will be needed for weighing the puppies, as will a clock, notebook and pencil, as you will most probably want to take notes whilst the puppies are being born.

Sterilizing tablets are essential, unless you have a proper sterilising machine, and scissors must be available in the whelping room, in case you need them to cut an umbilical cord; they should be blunt-ended and sterilised, ready for use. A premature-baby bottle is also necessary, in case you need to hand-feed any of the puppies. I find a 'prem-baby' bottle much the easiest kind to use and, if not available from your vet, you should be able to purchase one from a chemist, GP or hospital. Powdered glucose should also be kept in stock, for this is useful to give nourishment to the bitch when mixed with her drinking water. It can also be used as a supplement to water if a very young whelp needs to be hand-fed but is still too young to take a milk substitute. There are many milk substitutes available and one of these should be bought prior to whelping, so that you have it to hand should it be needed. Should prolonged hand-feeding be necessary it is wisest to stay with the same brand, so as to avoid upsetting the puppies' stomachs.

Chapter Eleven

WHELPING

It is of the utmost importance that you are clear in your mind and know exactly what to do when your bitch whelps. If you have not whelped a bitch before, or even if you have, it is wise to have read and re-read as much as possible about the subject. Keep an informative book in the whelping room, for it is only too easy, in a moment of crisis, to forget what the book said.

There are various different theories about giving a bitch additional calcium and this is something you may like to discuss with your vet. Some breeders commence before the litter is due, but I do not now give liquid calcium until immediately after the litter has been born.

APPROACHING WHELPING DAY
Shortly before a bitch is due to whelp, her temperature will drop, and many breeders like to take their Shar Pei's temperature for guidance as to when the time is approaching. However, there are equally many who do not feel comfortable doing this, and there are other signs by which you can be guided.

If you have had sound practical instruction on how to take a temperature and feel that you will not upset your bitch by doing so – there are now some safe, digital thermometers available, which are easy to read – you should begin on the fifty-seventh day, when it should be somewhere between 100 degrees and 101.4 degrees fahrenheit. You can then be on the look-out for a drop in temperature. Readings should be taken frequently, so that you know exactly when the drop begins, at which point shivering commences. Then the temperature will rise again, possibly up to as much as 102 degrees, and this is the point at which you should expect the bitch to begin pushing. If your bitch's temperature has dropped below 99 degrees and has remained constant for more than twenty-four hours, without further signs of labour, you must consult your vet.

Whether or not you take her temperature, it is equally important to observe your bitch's outward signs, as by no means all Shar Pei whelp on the due date. As I have said, a bitch can whelp, often without problem, as much as one week early, and so you should keep a very careful eye on her from this time on. Do not allow her to go outside to relieve herself alone. Natural instinct may cause her to decide she would like to make her den under a bush in your garden and, if your garden is large, you just could have problems finding her – and perhaps her puppies!

Expect your Shar Pei bitch to refuse food for anything between a few hours and a full day before she actually whelps. This is quite normal. She may also vomit slightly but this is no cause for concern unless she vomits to excess, in which case you should contact your vet. Over the preceding few days she will most probably have been nest-making in a half-hearted manner; by this time she should have become familiar with her whelping quarters. As the day and hour approaches, she will work harder and harder at making her nest, hopefully in the whelping box, for instinct will have told her that the time to whelp is rapidly approaching.

Her teats will probably have begun to fill with milk and she is likely to be restless. Especially if it is to be her first litter, she may follow you around more than normal and look to you for comfort. She will also begin to pant before she starts pushing. This can go on only for a short while or, sometimes, for several hours.

THE WHELPING

Shortly before the first whelp is produced, your Shar Pei bitch will frequently turn around to lick her vulva. You may not even have noticed that her waters have broken, for little water may have come away and she will have been busy checking herself in this area. By now a clear, white mucous discharge will have been produced from her vulva, which will have softened. If she is losing any deep colour at this stage, consult your vet at once. Sooner or later you will see her strain visibly, indicating that there is movement of puppies along the birth canal. It is likely that, during the last few days of pregnancy, you will have been able to feel the puppies moving around in her abdomen but this movement will have quietened down during the last couple of days before this, the second stage of labour, begins. Note the time of her first major strain and you should expect the strains to increase in frequency until the first puppy is pushed out. It is usual to have a gush of fluid prior to a bubble appearing at the vaginal entrance. The bubble will indicate that the puppy is still encased in its sac, a good sign. After a couple more strong pushes, the puppy should appear, still probably encased in the sac and attached by the umbilical cord to the placenta. Should it be that your bitch has been pushing for about an hour and a half to no effect, a call to your vet would be in order.

Shar Pei are usually adept at breaking the sac themselves, so you may not need to intervene and, indeed, you should only do so when absolutely necessary. However, sometimes, especially for the first whelp from a bitch's first litter, the bitch will need your assistance. Your main aim must be to give the new-born whelp the freedom to breathe, so the sac should be broken at the head end. The bitch will most probably also have severed the umbilical cord but, should she not have done so, this is something which you will need to do. Before tearing it (or cutting it with your blunt-ended, sterilised scissors) squeeze the blood supply up towards the puppy. I have never found it necessary to tie the umbilical cord but, if it bleeds profusely, squeeze it hard and, if necessary, tie with a piece of cotton thread about one inch from the body of the whelp, applying a drop of iodine to the cut end. Return the puppy immediately to the dam.

If the bitch is doing most of the work herself she will, almost certainly, try to eat the placenta, which is full of nutrients. Even if you are assisting, she may realise that the odd afterbirth is on offer and partake. I like my bitches only to eat two or three of these, as they have a laxative effect, so, when possible, try surreptitiously to take a few away. However, she has probably not eaten for a good few hours and may not wish to eat for the next few hours at least, so, if she has a couple of placentas inside her, I think that is a good thing. Always count the placentas as they come out of the bitch, for there are times when they become detached from the puppy and you need to be sure that all have been expelled by the end of the whelping session.

The bitch will, most probably, immediately lick and stimulate her new-born puppy herself but, if she does not, rub the pup briskly with a clean rough towel, holding the head downwards to drain off any fluid from the lungs. The mouth can then be gently swabbed out, with a piece of soft gauze pad, to remove any mucus. If you have not whelped a litter of puppies before, you will probably be horrified by the rough way in which a dam treats her puppies when they are first born. Obviously, you need to be there to make sure that things are not getting too rough, but it is surprising how much these little puppies can take! Something I try to watch carefully is that the

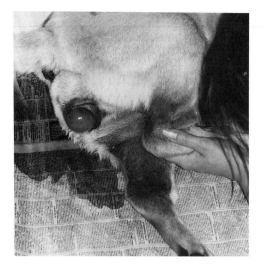

Birth is imminent: At this stage the puppy is still enclosed in the water bag.

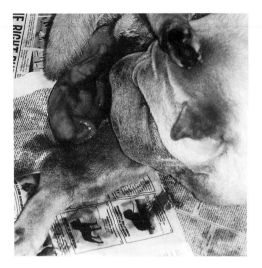

The water bag bursts and the puppy is born.

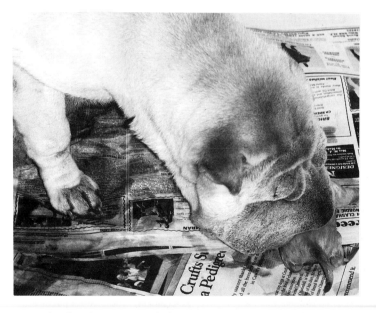

The dam breaks the umbilical cord with her teeth and then licks the puppy to clean and stimulate it .

All photos: Bill Lilley

The newborn puppies are now suckling from their mother.

Photo: Bill Lilley.

dam does not tug too fiercely on the umbilical cord in her endeavours to break it, as this can cause a hernia, though it may be only a temporary one which will disappear after a week or two. If she is being unduly rough in this regard, I always prefer to tear, or cut, the cord myself.

If there is time, before the next puppy is born, I like to make sure the latest arrival is already on a teat. Some will manage this automatically, others need encouragement by having you choose the juiciest-looking teat, gently squeezing out a little milk and holding the puppy onto it. The dam rarely seems to object to this help but may try to encourage the puppy in her own way too.

By the time the bitch is ready to produce her next whelp (this could be in as few as five minutes or as long as a couple of hours) she will be concentrating almost one hundred percent on the job in hand and this will be your first opportunity to take a quick look at the previous puppy. I like to be sure that all the new-born puppies are removed to the safety of the warm cardboard box during the process of delivery of a whelp, for that keeps them out of danger whilst the bitch is pushing. One or more puppies can be returned to the bitch between times so that she does not miss them. Remember that they should be covered with a light-weight, clean towel to stop them crying in the box, for their cries will disturb her.

While the whelping process is going on, I usually manage to find time to weigh the puppies and to make brief notes about the colour and sex of each one. At this point I also check for cleft palate, for, if not discovered now, with your own, scrupulously clean, finger, it can go undetected until the puppies start to take solid food – far too late if the decision has to be taken to have the puppy put down. When weighing the puppies, it is essential that the scales are somewhere safe, for even tiny puppies can wriggle about and fall off. I like to have my scales and notebook on the floor.

The average number of puppies for a Shar Pei bitch to produce is between three and five but it could be just one or, maybe, as many as ten. You will probably see a change in your bitch when she has finished whelping, for she will settle down and appear to be comfortable again. Do, though, check that there are no lumps or any bumps still inside her and, if you are at all unsure as to whether there is a puppy, or placenta, retained, you should consult your vet.

Before we go on to look at the various difficulties which might be encountered, let me say how important it is that all the puppies have at least some of the dam's first milk supply, which contains protective antibodies. Ideally, all puppies should have taken a drink by the time the last whelp is produced. Do be sure that they are actually drinking and not just hanging on to a teat, as some are prone to do. If you are lucky, all will have gone smoothly and the dam will have the puppies lined up in a row, drinking contentedly. Time for you to relax a while and let the bitch have a little rest.

THE NEW-BORN PUPPIES

Despite the fact that the older Shar Pei puppy will look quite different from other dogs, at birth the difference in not so great. Birth weight varies, as it does in any breed, but twelve to thirteen ounces seems about average. When the puppies first emerge from the dam, there are few or no wrinkles. These begin to develop at around two or sometimes three weeks of age and will continue to increase up to the age of four months. From this time on the puppies will 'grow into their skin', so that the wrinkle disappears again to a certain extent. From birth it is the distinctive nose of the Shar Pei which is most evident and it is usually possible to determine whether the puppies are born with horse, or brush, coats.

All Shar Pei are born with pink tongues, though some may have a small dot of pigment on the tongue or on the nose; pigmentation begins to appear properly when the puppy is about a week old. Those which are born with a spot of pigment often have the darkest pigment in adulthood, and in these it seems to fill in somewhat sooner than in those born without. It can take anything between three weeks and four months for the pigment to fill in completely. However, if a tongue has remained predominantly pink by the age of eight weeks, it may not change further.

A black or cream puppy is the easiest colour to determine at birth. Creams are born white and, provided there is some pigmentation on ears, nose, feet or pads, the puppy born white is not an

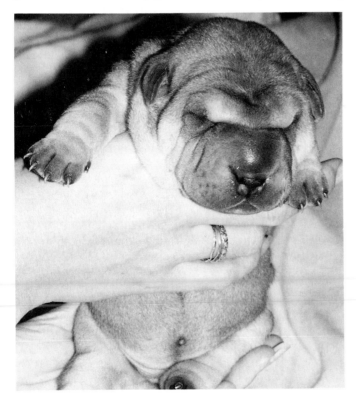

At a few days old, a Shar Pei puppy is beginning to acquire its distinctive looks.

Photo: Bill Lilley.

albino. Puppies born white usually darken quickly, becoming cream, and their ears have a distinctive apricot hue. Do not be confused, at this early stage, between a solid-coloured dog with darker shading or mottling and one which is a flowered or spotted puppy – the latter should be easy to pick out. Other colours are not easy to evaluate at birth and will either lighten, or darken, as the puppies grow older – a fawn may become a red, or a red become a fawn – but after six months the colour is unlikely to change very much.

You can expect your Shar Pei puppies' tails to be straight at birth but they should start to curl at about three weeks, or later. By eight weeks your puppies will, hopefully, carry their tails over their backs.

ABNORMAL WHELPINGS
Whilst it will be appreciated that it is not possible to give intricate details of the various types of abnormal whelpings, the following information may be of assistance:-

Inertia: This can occur in either the first or second stages of labour and, without going into great detail, it involves the bitch's lack of ability to produce her whelps. Primary inertia will preclude her from actually going into labour at all, possibly as the result of a very small litter, which does not generate sufficient hormone, or of a large litter resulting in an over-stretched uterus, which does not begin to contract. Secondary inertia occurs when she has started to whelp but then stops trying to expel the whelps, either because the uterus has stopped contracting or because she has simply tired herself out. Clearly if there is an exceedingly long delay between puppies, your vet will need to be consulted and, if the problem cannot be solved by some other means, a Caesarean operation will be performed to release the remaining whelps.

Malpresentation of a whelp: Not all puppies present head first, but those which do are the easiest ones for the bitch to expel. In Shar Pei, as in other breeds, as many as forty per cent of the litter can present feet-first. Provided that the spine of the puppy is uppermost, this is not a breach birth and rarely creates any problem. A breach is when the puppy is hind legs first and upside down, which is more difficult to expel. Occasionally a puppy will be presented sideways on and will need to be turned. Inexperienced breeders will certainly need to consult their vets in such circumstances but, for the more experienced, it may well be possible to turn the whelp to facilitate the birth. Under no circumstances should one pull at the whelp unless the bitch is pushing, so timing is of the utmost importance. If ever a puppy is pulled – and this must be done with expert timing and care – the pull must be in a downwards direction.

Still-born puppies: Occasionally, especially in cases where too much time has been spent in the vaginal tract, a puppy will be still-born. Provided that you are confident that the puppy is otherwise 'perfectly' formed and has only recently expired through lack of oxygen, you can certainly try resuscitation, but you must act quickly, preferably somewhere out of sight of the bitch. Clear the airways, as you would do normally, and rub the puppy's back and chest briskly with a rough, warm towel. If you are very lucky, you will have instant success; but if not, take the puppy firmly in both hands, one supporting the back of the head and the other the back and rear end. With the puppy's head facing downwards and making sure that the tongue is well forward, swing the puppy through the air, up and down, between your legs. If you still fail to meet with success, a drop of neat brandy on the tongue or, alternatively, the use of smelling salts, may just make the puppy gasp and thus begin to breathe. Although I have never used the latter method, I can see that it might well work, for I did once revive a dead mouse with dry white wine! Some people suggest breathing into the puppy's mouth but I do not advocate this method, for it is difficult to ascertain how much air the puppy's lungs are capable of taking. If you find that the tongue is white, indicating that the puppy has been dead for a longer period, it would not be wise to attempt resuscitation, for prolonged lack of oxygen will have caused damage to the brain.

Retained Placentas: It is important that you count the placentas expelled by the bitch for, whether or not you have allowed her to eat any of them, you will need to know that all have come away. If any have been retained, this can set up infection. Should you be unsure whether or not all have been expelled, you should discuss this with your vet who will, probably, give an injection to expel any which may remain.

CAESAREAN SECTION

If things do not go smoothly, the ultimate decision as to whether or not a Caesarean operation is carried out will rest with your vet. However, do not be afraid to discuss this with him in full, so that you are completely aware of why it needs to be done and when. Vets' opinions vary as to how soon after the due date an operation needs to be performed. I know of those who are anxious to operate when a bitch is three days overdue and others who are not unduly concerned if the puppies have still not arrived a week late. A lot depends on the circumstances and, of course, the condition of your bitch. Whilst the danger of losing one's bitch during such an operation is relatively low these days, any operation carries with it some element of risk, and this factor is increased if she is already exhausted from her attempts to produce the litter on her own. The decision must, therefore, not be taken lightly. The prime reasons for a Caesarean operation are:-

Malpresentation: A puppy in a position which precludes any normal passage through the birth canal. This can also block the way for subsequent puppies and can cause danger to the dam.

An exceptionally large puppy: The puppy is so large that the bitch is unable to expel it. This can sometimes be because the puppy is a singleton (a litter of one).

Uterine inertia: This is a lack of visible contractions, even though other signs of the birth process are evident.

A long, exhausting labour: The bitch may have produced some, but not all, of the puppies. As a result, she will gradually have weakened to such an extent that uterine and abdominal contractions have ceased.

Abnormal pelvic aperture: This could be due to a previous pelvic fracture or to a construction of the hindquarters which is such that she would, in any event, have difficulty in passing puppies normally. If there is any doubt as to a bitch's suitability for breeding, she should be checked over by a vet before the decision is taken to have her mated. In the case of any previous accident in which there was injury to the pelvis, there is always a danger of internal trouble, even though there are no outward signs of damage.

POST-OPERATIVE CARE

When a Caesarean operation has been performed, your bitch should be totally alert by the time she once again reaches home. Her puppies must not be returned to her until she is fully conscious because, when a bitch has not actually gone through the process of whelping (except in cases where she has actually produced one or more of the whelps herself), it may well take her longer than usual to accept the puppies. It is, therefore, a good idea to return them to her one at a time, so that she is not totally confused by the entire litter. Try to get each puppy, in turn, to take some of her milk, as the colostral antibodies will only be present in her milk supply for between twenty-four and forty-eight hours. She will need rather special care – and you will need to keep an eye on her when she goes out to spend a penny, in case she pops any of her stitches. Soon the bitch will treat her puppies as though she has had a normal delivery, and you will be surprised how she tolerates the kneading of the puppies' feet on her tender stomach.

There are cases when a bitch who has had one Caesarean is able to whelp another litter quite

In the first few days following birth the puppies will spend all the time either eating or sleeping, and their dam will care for all their needs. Note the different coat textures and colours.

Photo courtesy: Linda Rupniak.

normally; but if she were to need a second, it would be most unwise to mate her again. Once she has had a Caesarean, it is essential that you discuss the matter fully with your vet before you consider mating her on a subsequent occasion.

POST-WHELPING

When the whelping is over, the bitch will be reluctant to be parted from her new litter, but a short while after you are certain that the last puppy has been produced, take her outside to give her the opportunity to relieve herself, although she will almost certainly be reluctant to do so. Stay with her whilst she is outside (just in case there is another whelp tucked up in the rib-cage) and give her a very quick freshen-up, especially around her back end, before she goes back to her puppies. Be sure that she is offered plenty of glucose water but don't expect her to get out of the whelping box for this; at this stage, she will most probably not want to leave her litter, even for a drink. Do not leave water in the box, for that is a possible danger to the young whelps. The bitch will not feel like eating yet, but I often find that my bitches are grateful for a whisked egg-yolk (do not give the white) mixed with a drop of milk and into which I conceal the first dose of liquid calcium. The calcium can also be syringed into the mouth if the bitch does not wish to eat the egg.

The bitch should, by now, be content to settle down with her litter but, if she is still showing signs of distress, you should contact your vet, for there is a chance that something is amiss, possibly the retention of a dead puppy. In any event, especially if you are inexperienced, it would be wise to have your veterinary surgeon check the bitch to see that everything is in order. He may decide to give an injection of pituitrin and, perhaps, antibiotics to help expel any placentas which might possibly remain and to speed up the contraction of the uterus. Bear in mind, however, that your bitch will not wish to be away from her puppies for too long, so it is probably worth the additional 'call out' fee to have your vet visit your home. If you have to go to the surgery, depending on its proximity, you will, most probably, need to take the puppies along as well. They should be transported in a secure cardboard box, with a wrapped hot-water bottle in the base, and they should be lightly covered with a clean towel; this will prevent them from crying. Make sure the vet knows that you are on your way so that you do not have to linger too long in the waiting room – especially during surgery hours – and do not be afraid to ask the receptionist for a top-up in the hot-water bottle so that the puppies have an equally comfortable journey home. Obviously consultation with a vet, at this stage, also gives the opportunity to have the puppies checked to make sure there is nothing wrong.

Chapter Twelve

CARING FOR THE LITTER

THE EARLY WEEKS

During the first couple of weeks the bitch will want to spend virtually all her time with the puppies, but that does not mean to say that she will not need to know that you are around in the background, ready to assist her should the need arise. Shar Pei puppies are usually fairly strong and robust but, at this stage, they are still completely dependent upon others for their needs. Sometimes, for example, a puppy may have strayed to a far corner of the box out of the dam's reach, and she will be reluctant to leave the rest of the litter if they are feeding. The puppy must, in such cases, be replaced on a teat, for a puppy will weaken and fail to survive if not fed at regular intervals.

In the first few days the dam will still be reluctant to get out of the box, even for a drink, so you will need to offer her glucose-water frequently. Food should be offered little and often, and, because her digestive system will be rather delicate for the first couple of days, she should be kept on a light diet of chicken or fish (both carefully boned, of course). I would also suggest giving two egg yolks whisked with milk each day, whilst she is still feeding the puppies. You will very probably have to coax her to eat during the first forty-eight hours and do not be afraid to hand-feed her, if that is the only way you can get her to take food. As soon as the novelty of her puppies wears off slightly, her appetite will return and she will readily leave the whelping box to eat her meals when they arrive.

It is normal for the bitch to have a mucous discharge from the vulva after the puppies are born. For the first couple of days this will be malodorous and dark, but the colour will then change to blood-red and will, eventually, pale off completely. This discharge is caused by bleeding from the surface of the uterus where the placentas have broken away. If the discharge remains thick and dark for more than a couple of days, your vet should be consulted without delay.

The room housing the bitch and her puppies should be kept at a constant temperature of about 75 degrees fahrenheit, or it can be a little cooler, provided that an infra-red lamp is being used to heat the whelping box itself, so that the puppies have additional heat. As I have already said, I prefer the latter arrangement, for the bitch can be free to move to somewhere a little cooler when not in with her puppies and, if the lamp is situated off-centre, she need not be in its direct rays.

Most bitches will settle down perfectly contentedly at this early stage, but some can take time to adjust and will persist in moving their puppies about from place to place. Such bitches, who thankfully are in the minority, will need to be kept in the whelping box (making sure they are not too hot); but, if they continue to be unsettled, a vet should certainly be consulted.

Weighing of the puppies should be done on a daily basis for the first couple of weeks so that you can be alert to any problems; you should expect a Shar Pei puppy to gain weight at upwards of two

A two-week-old litter of the 'old style'. The puppies have rather large, low-set ears, but they are of a good size with typical expression and good pigment.

Photo: Bill Lilley.

At fifteen days old this puppy's eyes are just opening. Note the black tongue is already evident.

Photo: Bill Lilley.

ounces a day, so that it has roughly doubled after two weeks. Weighing should be done while the bitch is out in the garden, so that she does not have to witness any undue disturbance to her precious charges. Hopefully, your puppies will all be putting on weight steadily (though there is, frequently, no increase during the first twenty-four hours); but, should it happen that any are not thriving as you would expect, check that the puppy is actually sucking and not just sleeping contentedly, attached to the teat. To help the puppy, you can supplement the diet by hand-feeding, and then let the bitch take over completely again when the proper weight and strength have been regained, thus giving the puppy the ability to compete with the rest of the litter.

When your bitch goes out for exercise, be sure that she does not come into contact with any ground which might carry infection from other dogs. You can expect her motions to be somewhat loose, for she will be cleaning up entirely after her puppies at this stage, licking tummy and anus to stimulate the flow of urine and bowel action. Always give her a quick check over before putting her back with her puppies, this being an opportunity to be sure that there are no signs of mastitis and that her discharge is clearing as it should.

Keep a dull light in the bitch's room throughout the night; this will enable her more easily to keep a check on the whereabouts of her puppies and will assist her if she needs to get out of the box for a drink, or a snack, during the night. Personally, I always like to sleep in the same room as my bitch and her puppies for the first ten days or so, just so that I am there if problems arise during the night.

MUSCLE TWITCHING
Do not be disturbed by the fact that the puppies seem to twitch a lot. Ninety percent of a new-born puppy's life is spent sleeping and muscle twitching is perfectly normal at this time, for it plays an essential part in the development of the muscles.

UMBILICAL CORDS
The umbilical cords should have dried up neatly within the first couple of days – they shrivel up and then fall off (possibly assisted by an over-indulgent dam!). Should there be any sign of infection in the navel, it should be bathed in a mild antiseptic and, if it fails to clear up quickly, or if there is any swelling, the vet should be consulted.

DEWCLAWS
The Shar Pei breed standard gives an option as to whether or not dewclaws should be left on a Shar Pei, but most breeders have them removed. The Chinese, though, say that to have five toes is a lucky sign. If they are not removed, puppy purchasers must be advised that dewclaws are present and that they will not wear down of their own accord as, to a certain extent, do the nails on the other toes. Under no circumstances must a puppy buyer be encouraged to have dewclaws removed at a later stage in the dog's life, for this is entirely unnecessary, unless there are exceptional circumstances, and will involve a general anaesthetic, which could otherwise be avoided. In recent years I have tended to leave dewclaws on and have come across no problems whatsoever. Some Shar Pei have double dewclaws, whilst others have none at all on the hind feet.

If you decide to have the dewclaws removed, possibly because it looks neater or because you are worried about injury by tearing, they must be removed by your vet at the age of three days or, certainly, no more than four. You may have heard it said that some breeders remove dewclaws themselves, but it is a skilled operation, which causes some pain, and must therefore only be done by a vet. Unless you have the vet out to your home, you will need to take the bitch along to the surgery with the puppies, for she will be frantic if they are taken away from her, even for a short

*Puppies pictured
at four weeks old:
weaning is now
under way.*

Photo: Bill Lilley.

period. It would be wise to give your vet a call to let him know that you are on your way, although he will, most probably, expect to remove dewclaws in surgery hours. If you are worried about infection which may be picked up in the waiting room, it will be perfectly in order for you to tell the receptionist that you have arrived and to wait outside in the car until it is your turn to see the vet. The bitch will have to be kept entirely out of ear-shot while the vet removes the claws, for the enormous noise the puppies make will disturb her considerably. Thankfully, their agony is short-lived and, with potassium permanganate, the bleeding is stopped almost instantly, so that they can go straight back to their dam.

EYES
The puppies will have been born with their eyes tightly closed, and so they will remain for about the first ten days. They will open of their own accord and on no account should they be forced, though if they are particularly sticky they may be bathed with a warm solution of very weak tea. At any sign of infection, the vet should be contacted immediately. Once they are open, the eyes will be a misty blue in colour and will not be able to focus properly. At this early stage the puppies should be kept away from bright light. The colour will clear and darken as the days progress.

Many breeders find that it is helpful to have the eyes of their young puppies tacked, something which is done in the early weeks of the puppy's life. This subject will be discussed in Chapter 13.

EARS
At birth the ears will also be sealed and these will, usually, have opened by the thirteenth to seventeenth day. You will need to wipe your Shar Pei's ears clean with cotton swabs, dipped in a little mineral oil, from roughly eighteen days onwards.

NAILS
Puppies' nails are sharp and seem to grow extremely quickly. For the comfort of the dam, and as a

measure of protection against injury to each other by accidental scratching, nails should be trimmed regularly with nail scissors.

PROBLEM PUPPIES

Dehydration: Dehydration, caused sometimes by loose stools, is a matter for concern. Undoubtedly if a puppy is limp when picked up, urgent veterinary attention is essential.

Poor suckers: The crying of a puppy may be an indication of insufficient milk. As has already been mentioned, the puppy will need individual attention, placing on a teat about every two hours with the suckling checked to make sure it is actually happening. Supplementary hand-feeding may be necessary.

Toxic milk supply: This is indicated by puppies who cry more than normal, may appear bloated and may suffer from greenish-coloured diarrhoea, with a red swollen anus. Your vet should be consulted immediately and the puppies will, very probably, have to be hand-reared, as infected milk is one of the causes of early death amongst puppies.

Lack of stimulation: Another reason for crying can be that the puppy needs to pass urine but has not been stimulated by the bitch to do so. You will have to do this on her behalf, simulating her washing action by rubbing the tummy and anus with a damp tissue. This will encourage the puppy to pass urine and to defaecate. The puppy should then be passed back to the bitch, rear end first and, in most cases, you will find that she will continue her maternal duties in the normal manner. In the unlikely event of your having a bitch who is reluctant to clean up after her puppies, it will probably help if you smear a little vegetable oil on the puppies, thereby giving her the stimulation to start cleaning them.

Umbilical hernias: If present, these will probably already have been noticed. I have already mentioned that they can have been caused by an over-zealous dam and, if the hernia is small, it will probably close up with the passage of time. However, the majority of umbilical hernias are hereditary and, as the puppy grows, the hernia will need to be checked by a vet to ascertain whether or not surgical rectification is necessary. Although many dogs can live a full life without any problem, there can be a danger of strangulation. The buyers of any puppies with hernias must have the problem pointed out to them and the full facts should be explained.

Sucking due to teething: Puppies begin to teeth at around three weeks, or sometimes earlier. At this time they will try to suck anything which is available and the choice of object is not always the bitch's teat. Accidents can happen when puppies suck the limbs, ears and penises of their siblings, and they must be discouraged from doing this before damage occurs.

Swimmers: 'Swimmers' appear as flat puppies, with caved in chests and legs extending out to the side, as if they are swimming a breast-stroke. When the rest of the litter starts to get on their feet, swimmers will not and will need your assistance. You need to handle them frequently and try to keep them on their sides, rather than on their tummies. In extreme cases, splints may have to be fitted to the legs. It seems that the reason for swimmers in a litter can be either nutritional or genetic, and it is believed that Vitamin C can be of some help. Provided that complications do not occur, full recovery is often possible.

Puppy pyoderma: At the age of around three weeks, some Shar Pei puppies may experience skin problems in the form of impetigo, or pyoderma. An iodine solution, rubbed on the affected spots, can often help to clear this up quite rapidly. Bathing with an iodine shampoo can also help. If the skin problem spreads, or does not clear up quickly, you must consult your vet. A vitamin programme can help build up an immunity but pyoderma in a puppy could be a sign that, when adult, this Shar Pei will continue to have skin problems.

Megaoesophagus: This is a condition in which the oesophagus is dilated and covers the path of the food from throat to stomach. It is not usually noticed until the early stages of weaning, when the puppy may vomit the food. This could well have been happening since birth, but you may not have noticed as the bitch will have kept the puppy clean, but it could be the cause of a puppy being slow to gain weight. Prognosis is poor and aspiration pneumonia can result but, occasionally, surgery can be of help. If the case is only mild, it can help the puppy if the feeding bowl is raised slightly from the ground. Megaoesophagus is believed to be inherited and such a puppy which survives should certainly never be bred from.

DECIDING WHEN TO START WEANING

By the time the puppies have reached three weeks of age, you should be handling them a great deal and the bitch will, hopefully, not object to you doing so. This is the time at which human contact is most important; it is also a particularly important week in the puppies' psychological development and should be free from unnecessary trauma. For this reason, and providing I feel the bitch is coping adequately with her litter and is not being over-drained, I prefer to begin to wean puppies in the fourth week, though many breeders do this at three weeks. However, the bitch's well-being must be the first priority and, if she has a large litter or seems otherwise unable to cope, weaning must start sooner. There are a number of conditions which might affect the bitch and will certainly influence your decision.

Mastitis: This will first be observed by one of the teats becoming hot, hard or inflamed. It will be sore and the bitch may, therefore, be distressed. If caught in the early stages, it may be rectified by holding a warm cloth over the affected teats and by trying to express a little of the milk by hand. If this appears to be working, hold the puppies to the affected teats and encourage them to use these teats rather than the others. Should hardening continue and the matter appear not to be resolved within the space of twelve hours, veterinary advice should be sought.

Metritis: The first sign of metritis in a bitch is a lack of interest in her puppies and a certain lethargy. Metritis is an inflammation of the uterus and the condition is usually caused by an unborn foetus, or a retained placenta. If caught in sufficient time it can usually be rectified with a course of antibiotics. If not treated, the milk will become toxic, and the puppies will have to be hand-reared.

In severe cases, and occasionally when the bitch does not respond to treatment, spaying may be necessary. Metritis can sometimes be fatal. It can also be caused by bacteria introduced into the genital tract, possibly by using unclean fingers to aid a difficult whelping or from unclean bedding. Scrupulous cleanliness is therefore essential.

Eclampsia: I find eclampsia one of the most frightening things which can happen to a bitch, for it can come about within such a short period of time, and death can occur within the space of a few hours. This is why it is essential to have sufficient time to spend with a bitch and her litter. In humans this is known as 'milk fever' and is often thought to be caused by lack of calcium but, in fact, it is due to the body's inability to transport the calcium from the body reserves into the bloodstream.

It is easy to miss the first outward signs of eclampsia: the bitch may seem a little strange and endeavour to nest-make, scratching up the bedding, much as she did shortly before she whelped. As the condition progresses, she will seem uneasy, restless and on edge, probably panting more than usual. If you place your hands on her shoulder blades at this stage, you may be able to perceive a slight tremble, which will soon develop into a shiver. Her legs will stiffen and she will begin to wobble about, having difficulty in standing. As her condition worsens, her pulse will become rapid and she will salivate, eventually going into convulsions, by which time her temperature will have risen to as much as 104 degrees (41 degrees C).

The only way to save the bitch is by a massive dose of calcium, given intravenously by your vet, so, whatever the time of day or night, do not delay. Ring the vet at once, telling him your suspicions of eclampsia, and let him know that you are on your way to the surgery as a matter of urgency. Once he has administered the calcium, your bitch will most probably seem to recover almost immediately, but that does not mean that she can necessarily continue to feed her puppies as she did before. On this matter you will have to take your vet's advice, which may vary, depending on the severity of her previous condition and the age and size of the litter of puppies. He may say that she cannot feed them at all, or may give strict instruction as to the maximum amount of time to be spent with the puppies each day, for, naturally, to be taken away from them completely causes great distress. In this case, it will very probably be necessary for you to supplement the puppies' feeds. Even if your vet permits her to continue feeding, it would be advisable to commence weaning as soon as possible.

WEANING

By about three weeks of age the puppies should be up on their feet and be starting to move around, their confidence growing daily. This is the time at which they will need a little more space, though they should still be kept safely enclosed so that they are out of harm's way. Electric cables, for example, can be lethal if a puppy decides to exercise new teeth on the rubbery taste of the outer casing! The dam will now choose to spend a little more time away from her litter, signifying that it is time for you to take over their general care and feeding.

Once the puppies are introduced to solid foods, she will no longer clean up after them and the dirty work will be left entirely to you. This is when your work really begins. You will need to encourage the puppies to urinate and defaecate outside their sleeping quarters, which they usually like to keep reasonably clean. I cover only half the surface of the whelping box with bedding, leaving just a good supply of newspaper on the other half. I usually find that, in most cases (there are always exceptions!), they use the newspaper, which, of course, needs to be changed with great regularity.

CHOOSING THE CORRECT FOOD

Every breeder has personal preferences as to the most successful way to wean and I am sure that we all experiment with new feeding products from time to time. There are now some excellent proprietary puppy feeds on the market and, if you choose these, I do feel it must be stressed that they are to be used strictly in accordance with the maker's instructions. It is also important to select a brand which you know you can get hold of easily, or else you should buy a large enough supply to last until the puppies are at least several weeks old. Changing the type of food given during the weaning process can cause havoc and will, almost certainly, cause upset tummies.

The metabolism of a Shar Pei is different from that of Western breeds but has, I believe, much in common with the Asiatic breeds of dog. One breeder has found that to wean using an adult formula, rather than a puppy feed, seems to work very well for the Shar Pei, because it is lower in protein. This is a diet of rice, lamb and a little fish, made up of no more than twenty-two per cent protein and fifteen per cent fat. Using this, she has not encountered any skin problems and feels that the bone, coat and general condition of the puppies progresses well.

It is much easier to commence weaning when the puppies' tummies are empty and they therefore feel hungry. For this reason, do not offer the food when they are already wide awake and have, probably, fed from their dam. Instead, wait until they awake from a nice long sleep, undoubtedly feeling hungry. I find that the ideal feeding bowl is shallow but large enough for all the puppies to get their heads into, without having to push one another out of the way. Of course, it must be a bowl which is easy to clean thoroughly; my own preference is for stainless steel.

The first feed is almost always a bit of a performance for, almost certainly, one little mite will decide to walk into the bowl whilst you are concentrating on someone else! However, I do find that those who commence weaning at four weeks take to it with rather more of a professional attitude than youngsters of only three weeks. But, after the first few feeds, all the youngsters seem to know exactly what they are doing and look forward to their meal-times with relish.

A WEANING SCHEDULE

The following weaning schedule is the one which I normally follow and one which seems to work well, though others may prefer a different food content. Naturally, in the early stages, the puppies will continue to feed from their dam between meals but their need to do so should wane as the weeks progress.

Day One: Introduce one milk feed around lunchtime; this should be a rather 'sloppy' mixture of good-quality oats, with warm goat's milk and a teaspoonful of clear honey. It is not advisable to change from one kind of milk to another; so, if fresh goat's milk is not readily available, it is worth knowing that it freezes well and can often be purchased, pre-frozen, from health food stores. Alternatively, there are several good proprietary milk mixes – but take care to select one designed especially for puppies, and mix up exactly as the instructions indicate.

Day Two: Feed a milk meal (as above) at lunchtime and another milk meal (also as above) just before bedtime. This will prevent the puppies from taking too much from the bitch during the night.

Day Three: Give a milk feed as soon as the puppies wake up in the morning, before they have had time to feed off the dam. At lunchtime, introduce their first meat meal of well-soaked puppy feed (put it through a blender for the first few days) with a top-quality brand of canned puppy meat, which is very well mashed. Another milk feed should be given just before bedtime.

Day Four and onwards: Breakfast and lunch should be as per day three. Next, give a milk feed in the late afternoon and another meat meal last thing at night, establishing a pattern of milk, meat, milk, meat.

QUANTITIES

It is really not possible to be specific about quantities; it will obviously vary according to the number and size of the puppies and the bitch's own milk supply. If the puppies do not clean up their bowl at each feed, it is much better to feed a little less at each meal, rather than to reduce the schedule to three meals. The bitch will gradually be spending longer and longer away from her charges and will, most probably, do this of her own choosing. If she is reluctant to leave them, you will need to encourage her to be away from them, in order that her milk supply begins to dry up. The puppies should be completely weaned by about seven weeks of age, so that they are capable of looking after themselves by the time they move on to their new homes. You will need to slowly reduce your bitch's intake of food, but it must still be of the very highest quality.

WORMING

Even though you will have wormed your bitch shortly prior to mating, there is still a possibility that the puppies will have worms, as the worm ova can be passed from the dam, via the placenta, to the unborn whelps. Worms in the adult may have lain dormant for years but hormonal change during pregnancy will have freed them. A worming programme should commence at about four weeks of age and the dam should also be wormed at this time.

Chapter Thirteen

HEALTH CARE

In my opinion it is essential that, if any breed of dog has problems which are inherent, they should be discussed openly, for only in that way can such defects be eradicated. It has, though, to be appreciated that the elimination of hereditary defects often takes many generations of breeding and still certain things crop up, quite unexpectedly, from time to time.

This is not a book about genetics, but nonetheless I feel it imperative that problems which one may or, hopefully, may not encounter, are at least highlighted in a breed book such as this. Some heath difficulties which are encountered by the Shar Pei are common to many breeds of dog; others are more specific to the Shar Pei and, in some cases, other related breeds. I hope, therefore, that this chapter will be read in the spirit in which it is written, to help breeders eradicate problems and to help owners to live as easily as possible with whatever problems they might encounter.

There is absolutely no point in burying one's head in the sand and hoping that unpleasant subjects will simply go away. They will not. It behoves all who love and have a genuine interest in the Shar Pei to help them lead lives which are trouble free. As breeders we 'play god'; it is surely then our duty to the dogs we create to see to it that, by careful research and by attention to breeding programmes and to the health-care products available, we enable them to live happy, healthy lives. I know that many breeders have worked hard to eliminate problems which have arisen; hopefully, even more people will follow suit.

Let me begin, therefore, with a subject which is currently causing much concern and yet one about which written information is not easily available.

SWOLLEN HOCK SYNDROME

This is also known also as Familial Shar Pei Fever and Systemic Amyloidosis. It is something which appears to be rearing its head more and more frequently amongst Shar Pei. For example, at the American specialty in 1991 it was revealed that between eleven and twenty-three per cent of Shar Pei had experienced it in some form.

It is thought to be an inherent disorder and, as far as research has been taken at present, it is most probably autosomal recessive. Without going into too much genetic detail here, this effectively means that a dog, though not showing any outward signs of the disorder, may still be carrying it, and so, when that dog is mated to another carrying the defective genes, puppies can be produced either with the syndrome or carrying it. It is therefore imperative that one checks into the background of dogs' pedigrees before deciding upon a mating plan; and it must surely go without saying that no dog which is known to have suffered such attacks should be used in a breeding programme. It is also imperative to eliminate from one's breeding programme any other close relatives which are known to have had or to have carried the syndrome. I recognise that this is a sweeping statement to make in a breed which is not yet numerically strong in countries such as the UK, but I feel it is essential to face up to the problem before it gets too great a hold.

It would be wise to have the kidneys and tissues checked of any Shar Pei which have died prematurely. This should show whether amyloid protein is present, so that one knows whether or not this particular problem has been one of the causes of death.

Hock Syndrome is caused by an inability to break down, and hence get rid of, amyloid protein, which instead builds up and, effectively, takes all life out of the kidney and liver. Consequently Shar Pei with chronic Hock Syndrome die from kidney or liver failure at an early age. Because the kidney is not an organ which regenerates itself, when damage is done it is there to stay. The amyloid can also deposit itself anywhere in the body, this being the reason why swollen legs can be one of the ways in which the syndrome is expressed.

Symptoms for which one should be on the look-out are lethargy, lack of appetite or, perhaps, a raging temperature combined with shivering, seemingly without reason and for which the vet can often find no apparent cause. Another outward sign can be that the Shar Pei's muzzle is swollen, looking rather as if there may have been a wasp sting, and the eyes may be puffed up. In such instances the dog may scream with pain when the muzzle is touched. Following an attack, the Shar Pei may lose its muzzle, but this will eventually return to normal.

Shar Pei which have been prescribed cortisone-based drugs for differing illnesses also have a tendency to lose muzzle. This means that they lose the padding on the muzzle, the tissue of which is made up of a good deal of fluid, and seems almost to melt away as the cortisone reduces the fluid content. In Shar Pei whose size of muzzle is based more on bone than on padding, the reduction in size is understandably less obvious. However, in the case of loss of muzzle due to cortisone treatment, the muzzle will gradually return to its former fullness when the course of treatment is complete.

Returning again to the subject of Hock Syndrome, there may also be stiffness in the joints and the Shar Pei may have difficulty in putting either, or both, hind legs on the ground. When walking, the dog may, perhaps, just use three legs and the back legs could well be swollen and thickened. Another sign, especially in puppies, is that the back may be roached abnormally due to abdominal pain, added to which there can be diarrhoea and vomiting.

The frequency with which attacks occur varies; some Shar Pei get just one or two such attacks during puppyhood and then not again for the rest of their lives. However, it must be stressed that, in such circumstances, your Shar Pei is affected with the syndrome and this must be taken into account in future breeding programmes. Other Shar Pei may have an attack as frequently as every week of their lives.

It is perhaps easy to mistake Shar Pei Hock Syndrome for a banged leg, pulled tendon or wasp sting, and it is, I regret to say, all too easy to accept this as the cause of an occasional attack, without investigating the problem more deeply.

In the young puppy, a significant temperature rise, to as much as 108%, could prove fatal, so it is necessary to monitor temperature regularly during an attack and to do one's utmost to keep this down. The usual age at which Hock Syndrome affects young stock is between four and eighteen months, though it has been known in puppies as young as eight weeks. There are other Shar Pei who experience no signs in their youth but have bouts of the syndrome during adulthood.

If you are unfortunate enough to experience such attacks in your Shar Pei, I feel sure it is helpful to know how best to deal with the circumstances, so as to alleviate as much discomfort as possible. Not having experienced this personally, the recommendations I make are those which have been passed on to me by those who have, and those who have carried out research on the subject. An aspirin or dispirin given to a Shar Pei in fever seems to work well and, as already mentioned, it is essential to keep the dog's temperature down to as near normal as possible. This can be done by bathing behind the ears with cold, damp cloths, and the Shar Pei should, of course, be kept in a cool quiet room, undisturbed by other dogs. Drinks of honey water are useful, but the dog should not be forced to eat food. Naturally, if there is any cause for concern that the temperature is rising too high, the vet should be consulted at once to avoid a fatality.

It has been found that those Shar Pei which have attacks frequently are best kept on a low protein diet, between sixteen to twenty per cent. Natural Sulphur is seemingly good for purification of the system and either dried or fresh parsley can assist the kidneys. In America Dr Linda Tintle is carrying out extensive research on Hock Syndrome and hopes, eventually, to create a test which will ascertain whether or not such a syndrome is present. She has already discovered that Colchicine, used to treat gout in humans, decreases the frequency and severity of fevers in many animals and that it tends to block the development of amyloidosis.

American Shar Pei enthusiasts across the country have achieved great success in raising funds for Amyloidosis, the amount now standing at over $20,000. Research at Cornell University is on-going and contributions towards the cost of this research continue to flow in steadily. Dr Tintle says that much work has been done because of generous donations from people who love Shar Pei. Progress is being made but it is a slow learning process, venturing into uncharted territory.

ENTROPION

Another problem from which the Shar Pei can suffer is entropion, something which again, for the good of the breed, it is essential to face up to so that it can, in future, be eliminated from breeding programmes. Although the incidence of entropion is now less frequent than it used to be, it is, regrettably, still a common problem in the Shar Pei; and even if a young puppy shows no sign of entropion, it may develop at a later age, even into adulthood. Looking back to the breed's earlier history, it is relevant to recall that the small eye was a 'feature' of the breed to avoid damage in a fight.

Entropion is, effectively, the rolling in of one or both eyelids, thereby causing constant irritation to the eye as the eyelashes come into contact with the cornea. Imagine yourself with that problem for a moment or two and you will realise how very uncomfortable it must be, causing the eyes to blink frequently and to water profusely. Although entropion does occur in other breeds, in the Shar Pei the cause is often due, primarily, to the excess wrinkle around the eyes. The severity of the problem clearly differs according to the bloodlines involved in breeding programmes. Some puppies suffer so badly that, at the age of about ten days, when their eyes should be beginning to open, they cannot open as they should.

It is therefore imperative that the Shar Pei's eyes should be watched carefully, especially during those early weeks and months of development. Any sign of discharge, blinking or rubbing at the eye with the paws, a sign of discomfort, is reason for an immediate visit to the vet for further investigation. Constant rubbing can lead to ulceration, causing still further problems, which we shall deal with shortly.

The most usual time for entropion to become evident is between two weeks and fourteen months and, though it may be mild or severe, the majority of Shar Pei seem to be affected to some degree. For this reason, a great many breeders have their puppies' eyes tacked in place.

In severe cases surgery to correct entropion is necessary. This involves removing an elliptical section of skin and the underlying muscle from those eyelids which are affected, then closing the gap with sutures.

Obviously it would be infinitely better for a Shar Pei not to need corrective surgery of this nature and so it behoves all breeders to look carefully at their breeding stock, so that the problem can eventually be eradicated as the breed develops. Entropion, if left untreated, will probably cause ulcers and can result in blindness.

EYE TACKING

This is a procedure used by many Shar Pei breeders as a precaution against entropion. Carried out by a qualified vet within the first few weeks of life, it involves rolling out the eyelid and suturing it in place. The sutures are left in for about two weeks, giving time for the wrinkles to smooth out, though the procedure may have to be repeated again later as the wrinkles change with maturity. Some breeders have eye tacking carried out a number of times, up to one year of age, when they find that their Shar Pei eventually out-grows the problem.

Eye tacks can become loose, at which time there is a risk that they may turn into the eye, doing damage, even rupturing the cornea. Therefore, if you do decide to have your Shar Pei's eyes tacked as a preventative measure, be certain to keep a careful check that the sutures are properly in place until it is time to have them removed by your vet.

Six-week-old puppies, some with their eyes tacked.

Photo: Bill Lilley.

ULCERS

Ulcers can be caused by dust and debris collecting in the eye, or by injury, whether or not entropion is present. At the first sign of an ulcer it is, therefore, important to contact your vet, so that some suitable eye drops or ointment can be prescribed. Use of the wrong drops or ointment, if ulceration is present, will serve only to exacerbate the problem. In such cases the eyes must be kept scrupulously clean, gentle bathing with warm water will help, and the use of artificial tears, obtainable from your vet, can also be of assistance.

ECTROPION

This is the opposite of entropion and it is indeed possible that, in the same eye, one eyelid is affected with one problem and the other with its opposite number. According to some vets, in such cases, if the entropion problem is corrected, the ectropion will usually improve of its own accord. In a Shar Pei affected with ectropion, the eyelids roll away from the eye or droop, exposing the conjunctiva, thereby giving too little protection and bringing about irritation. Artificial tears again are of some assistance in alleviating the problem.

SWOLLEN HARDERIAN GLANDS

This is also known as 'Cheery Eye', though some vets consider it more correctly described as enlargement of the nictitating membrane. This condition is apparent when one notices a swollen gland in the inner corner of the eye. It can affect one eye or both, not necessarily at the same time. The gland is pink or pale red in colour and some vets try to treat it just with drops. However, I have found that this rarely seems to work long-term.

The swollen gland often appears and then disappears again, sometimes for months, but eventually it is there to stay. Vets used simply to lift the gland and snip it off to remove it completely, but this is not now considered the best method, for complete removal of the gland affects tear secretion. Tucking of the gland is an alternative procedure, introduced to the UK only a few years ago, and this seems to work well, though it may not always be successful, in which case complete removal has to be resorted to in the end and artificial tear drops should be used.

The gland usually appears between eight and twenty weeks, but I have known it as late as ten months. I have also had a single case of the gland appearing for just a day or two prior to, or following, a bitch's season – an interesting variation.

DRY EYE

This arises from insufficient tear production. If the eye is not properly lubricated, ulceration can occur, so artificial tear drops are usually necessary to keep the problem under control. A relatively new treatment, which has been used in human eye cases and is now available on the veterinary market, is cyclosporine. This is mixed with either olive oil or corn oil (which seems to irritate less) and is applied as one would use any other drops. Though more expensive than other eye drops, it is extremely effective and needs less frequent application. Just on the market as I write this is a new product which incorporates cyclosporine in an ointment. While it is even more expensive than the drops, I have found it works equally well and irritates the eye less.

Clearly, if the lacrimal secretion has been interfered with through surgery, dry eye can result, though probably no signs are noticed until several years later. It is therefore wise to apply artificial tear drops anyway, in an attempt to alleviate the problem.

TIGHT LIP

'Tight lip' is a condition specific to some Shar Pei because of the padding on the muzzle. If the padding is excessive, the lower lip can roll up and over the lower teeth. If this condition is present, you will find it virtually impossible to lower the bottom lip to expose the bite. This causes two problems. Firstly, difficulty and discomfort to the dog while chewing food and, secondly, it can cause pressure on the lower teeth, gradually pushing them backwards so that the Shar Pei ends up with an overshot mouth. I understand that surgery can be employed so that the dog can live a more comfortable life, although such a Shar Pei should never be used in a breeding programme and should not, of course, be shown.

ELONGATION OF THE SOFT PALATE
This sounds somewhat disconcerting but most Shar Pei suffer from this to a certain degree and indeed it is common, to a limited extent, in many relatively short-nosed breeds. Providing that the dog in question has no problems breathing and eating and does not tire easily, there is no cause for concern, though slight elongation can cause a Shar Pei to snore, a problem which the listeners will just have to live with! Obviously, if elongation of the soft palate causes any problems other than this, your vet must be consulted and surgery, involving taking out the excess tissue, will probably be recommended.

STENOTIC NOSE
This is a condition in which, when the puppy inhales, the nostrils are compressed, thereby closing the air passages. Bubbles may be blown from the nose after even minimal exercise. Surgery used to correct this problem involves removal of part of the nose or nostril. Clearly this is a very serious problem and one which breeders should be careful to avoid. Certainly no affected stock should be bred from or shown.

EAR INFECTION
Because of the smallness of the Shar Pei's ears and ear canals, there is a risk of bacteria building up and of consequent ear infection. The folded ear can prevent air from circulating and so it is necessary to check ears frequently for any sign of a waxy build up. There are now proprietary ear-cleaning fluids available, though it is important not to delve too deeply inside the ear. A dark, waxy discharge indicates the presence of ear mites, and a yellowish colour, with a bad odour, could possibly indicate a severe infection. In both cases, veterinary attention is needed so that some medication can be obtained to alleviate the problem as quickly as possible, for an infected ear causes a dog a good deal of discomfort, which is often apparent from the way the head is held, or if the dog constantly shakes it.

HAEMATOMA
A dog with discomfort in the ear may also scratch at the ear and cause a haematoma. This is when the blood vessels are broken, causing the ear flap to fill with blood, thus creating a swelling which may require surgical treatment. Care must be taken that a deformed ear does not result.

SKIN PROBLEMS
Skin problems can affect any breed of dog but, in the Shar Pei's formative years of re-development, the breed does seem to have had more than its fair share. This is due in part to the wrinkled skin. Should the feet, for example, be wrinkled, many Shar Pei will suffer from a certain soreness between the toes and also inside the pads of the feet. In such cases it is helpful to keep your Shar Pei away from damp surfaces, and a medicated powder, such as that used for athlete's foot, should be applied to the affected areas to provide relief. Chewing or licking of the feet,

sometimes the consequence of lack of exercise, will also cause problems because of the moisture from the dog's mouth.

SHAR PEI RASH

Hair loss occurs in patches and the dog looks vaguely 'moth-eaten', with red inflamed skin beneath. This may be due to reaction to the Shar Pei's own prickly hair, which irritates the skin. In some cases the hair loss affects the entire body. Referred to by some sources as Shar Pei Syndrome, it appears that tests which have been implemented in attempts to locate the problem have proved negative and, unfortunately, the symptoms do not usually respond well to treatment.

DERMATITIS

Something which can be found in any breed, dermatitis is a general term used for skin inflammation. This can have a variety of causes – allergies, parasites or hypothyroidism being some. There are occasions when a Shar Pei will simply grow out of any skin problems which may occur during the early months; in other cases they become chronic. Dermatitis seems to be more prevalent in the short, horse-coated Shar Pei than in those with brush coats. While in the early years of the breed's re-development in the West, skin disorders were frequently found, this is lessening with the passage of time, thanks to the careful breeding programmes which have been employed.

DEMODECTIC MANGE

Also known as red mange, demodectic mange is the commonest type of mange found in the Shar Pei. It is caused by parasitic mites, which thrive in the hair follicles of a dog with an inability to resist them, which is an inherited characteristic. The earliest visible sign of demodectic mange is the appearance of small patches without hair. These in time become reddened and then scaly, sometimes developing to open sores. In mild cases the dog's natural immunity may step in and reverse the procedure, or it may be reversed by early treatment. It is important to seek rapid medical advice, for, if it is allowed to become generalised, the dog's immune system can be depressed and illness result.

ALLERGIES

It is often very difficult to cope with allergies because it can be extremely difficult to isolate the actual source. Various tests are now available and it is wise to seek veterinary advice in an endeavour to pin-point the cause of the problem. The most usual symptom of allergic reaction is scratching and 'hot spots', caused by an infection under the skin, which can be exacerbated and opened by licking, in an effort to relieve discomfort. Such patches become hairless and moist, but your vet will be able to recommend something to dry them out and hence relieve the irritation. A flealess environment is, in any case, essential, but even more so in the case of a Shar Pei suffering from a skin complaint or allergy, as some can be especially sensitive to flea bites. It is worth noting that several of the Asian breeds are intolerant of dairy products, so this is something else which can be part of a trial elimination in one's endeavour to find the cause. According to Dee Gannon, a haemorrhoid ointment which contains an anti-inflammatory agent, as well as zinc, has proved useful in what she describes as "some of the mystery ailments such as hairless ears". Clearly it is wise to check with your vet before using such treatment.

ANAL GLANDS

Impacted anal glands can cause great discomfort for any dog. There are various theories as to

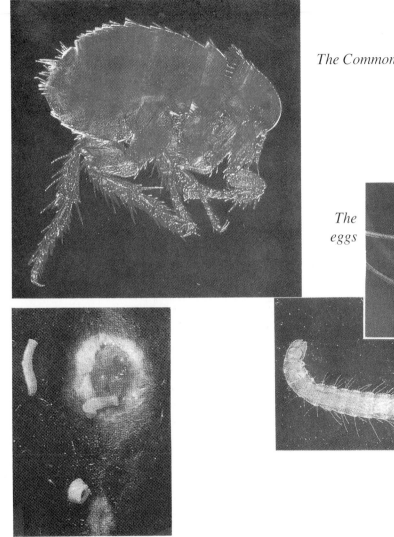

The Common Flea

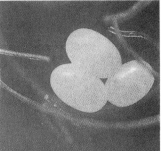

The eggs

The larva

Tape Worm segments

A preventative programme should be adopted to keep your dog free from parasites such as fleas and tapeworms.

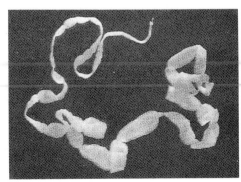

The Tape Worm can reach lengths of up to 20 inches.

Shar Pei are prone to sun-burn, and so some measure of protection must be found on hot days.

Photo: Carol Ann Johnson.

whether or not anal sacs should be emptied by a dog's owner on a regular basis. Personally this is something I have always done routinely, about every six weeks, and I have never yet experienced impacted glands nor any other problem as a result of frequent emptying. The glands are located one either side of the anal opening, just fractionally lower down, and can be felt as two approximately hazelnut-sized glands when full. To empty, cover the anus with a tissue, for there will be a foul-smelling brown-coloured discharge which is prone to shoot out unexpectedly, and gently squeeze the glands with the thumb and forefinger, placed in an upwards direction. Provided the glands are not impacted, and there is no abscess, this causes no discomfort to the dog. You must not squeeze too hard and, if you suspect that the glands are full but nothing is being evacuated, it would be best to get your vet to check.

A Shar Pei with impacted glands will show signs of discomfort by scooting on the backside along the ground (this can also be a sign of severe worm infestation). If the discharge is cream in colour, rather than brown, it may indicate that infection has already set in, so you will need to

Ir. Ch. Taiyattangs Silk Stockings: The mark of quality – the result of a careful breeding programme, good rearing, and detailed attention to adult care and maintenance.

Photo: Carol Ann Johnson.

Dog ownership can cause terrible heartache. This puppy, Konishiki Gift From God, died at the age of twelve weeks because the lungs were not properly formed.

Photo courtesy: Linda Rupniak

obtain antibiotics, probably in the form of an ointment, from your vet. In severe cases an abscess is likely to form, which will be noticed by the skin reddening and swelling in the anal area and the Shar Pei will, almost certainly, indicate pain in this region. In such cases your vet must be consulted so that appropriate medication can be given. Of course, if you prefer not to empty anal sacs yourself, this can be done quite routinely by a vet.

ABSCESSES

Abscesses can form on any part of the body, sometimes as the result of a tiny injury which may have gone unnoticed. These can usually be brought to a head by bathing gently in warm water until the abscess bursts and the pus evacuates. However, it is necessary that the place of evacuation is not allowed to heal over for a few days so that all the bad matter escapes. It is therefore wise to continue to bathe in hot water, putting gentle pressure on the sore place, in a downwards direction, to assist any discharge. Obviously if an abscess seems not to be clearing quickly, veterinary attention will be necessary.

RECTAL PROLAPSE
This can occasionally happen in the Shar Pei and must not be confused with an anal abscess. A prolapse of this kind protrudes from the anus as an inflamed mass and there may also be blood. This is usually caused by the dog having strained to defaecate but may also be the result of prostate disease in males, difficulties during the birth process in bitches, or by urinary obstruction or infection. Clearly veterinary attention must be sought urgently.

IMMUNE DEFICIENCY
This is a condition in which a puppy has a high fever without apparent reason, and it appears to be carried in some lines of Shar Pei. The immune system is depressed and does not respond as would be expected, though sometimes it appears simply to pick up of its own accord as a youngster matures. In severe cases, where the system is greatly depressed, there may be serious health problems and there often seems to be a susceptibility to demodectic mange.

MEGAOESOPHAGUS
In this condition the oesophagus dilates, the result of which is that water and food do not travel as they should do, directly to the stomach. This can often be detected at the weaning stage, as food is frequently regurgitated and there is slow weight gain. The condition can vary in degree but, in severe cases, aspiration-pneumonia may result and the prognosis for recovery is regrettably not good.

THYROID
Thyroid problems are known to several breeds and the Shar Pei is no exception. The most common problem of this sort appears to be hypothyroidism, involving a low thyroid output. Symptoms are lethargy, lack of stamina and coats which are sparse and dry. The skin may also darken in colour and become thicker. These symptoms most frequently begin to appear between the ages of two and about five years, and blood tests are available to determine the concentration of thyroid hormones in the system. Hypothyroidism is believed to be genetic, but treatment is available and is usually successful.

HIP DYSPLASIA
Several breeds of dog suffer from hip dysplasia, some more badly than others. Hip dysplasia, known as HD, arises when the head of the femur does not fit neatly into the hip socket, so allowing more movement in the joint than is correct in a well formed hip joint. This can give rise to continuous pressure on the joint, resulting in calcium deposits being formed and both inflammation and arthritis can result. HD can be diagnosed by X-ray and the severity differs quite considerably from dog to dog and from hip to hip. In severe cases it is both painful and crippling, whilst those affected less severely can often lead a normal life with little pain. There has been a wealth of study in this field and, if your vet suspects HD in your Shar Pei, he will almost certainly be able to guide you in the right direction. It goes without saying, I hope, that Shar Pei with severely defective hips should not be used in breeding programmes.

LUXATING PATELLA
This can be an hereditary problem or is, occasionally, caused by injury. The patella, or kneecap, normally held in position by muscle and tissue, slips out of place because these have weakened. In hereditary cases it is clearly wise to consider eliminating such an animal from any Shar Pei breeding programme.

If you plan to show your puppy, problems such as travel-sickness must be overcome at an early stage, as show-going, particularly in North America, involves travelling long distances.

Photo: Carol Ann Johnson.

CARPAL LAXITY

In carpal laxity there is a weakness of the carpal ligaments, causing instability in the 'wrist' of puppies. This may bow forward. The likely causes of carpal laxity are over-nutrition, rapid growth or inadequate exercise.

OTHER GENERAL PROBLEMS

Before closing this chapter it may be helpful to highlight some other problems which can be encountered by any dog and which can be cause for concern.

Many people do not consider that dogs can be affected by hay fever as humans can, and yet often if a dog has watering eyes, sneezing and inflammation of the mucous membranes, this might just be the cause. It is not always easy to find some means of relief but, with the assistance of your vet and some degree of patience, using trial and error, it is usually possible to find something to alleviate the problem.

Sneezing can also be caused by membranes within the nose being inflamed due to an irritant such as a grass seed, slight injury or even a parasite. If sneezing persists, a vet must be consulted without delay and it should also be borne in mind that it can be a sign of a serious illness such as distemper.

Fortunately I believe that all dog owners are now more aware of heatstroke than they used to be, partly because of the many disturbing announcements one hears over the speaker systems at shows, when strict warnings are given to those who leave dogs in cars. It is surprising how quickly heat can build up in a car, even on a relatively mild day with windows slightly open. Time is of the essence when treating heatstroke. The dog should be placed in the cool and have either iced or very cold water liberally applied to head, neck and shoulders. No attempt must be made to give the unconscious dog a drink but, when consciousness has been regained, glucose water or a light saline solution can be offered.

The initial signs of poisoning are various but can include sudden vomiting, muscular spasms and, in the case of warfarin poisoning, bleeding from an exit point such as the gums. The antidote administered will depend upon the type of poison taken, so it is of great help to your vet if you can give details of the source of poisoning. It is worth remembering that a dog can not only eat poison but can also walk on it and lick it from the pads of the feet. Telephone your vet immediately, giving as much information as possible and he will tell you whether or not vomiting should be induced. Your Shar Pei will be best kept warm and quiet, but with a little fresh air.

A sting can be a frightening experience both for dog and owner, and stings in the mouth or on the throat can be dangerous, needing urgent veterinary attention by way of anti-histamine injection. A dog which has been stung in this area should be kept cool and the tongue should be kept forward, so that the airway remains clear. The most usual place for a sting is on the pad of the foot and this is much less serious, albeit no less painful. Various proprietary medicines are available which will usually bring some relief, and vinegar is particularly good for wasp stings. Bicarbonate of soda can be applied to bee stings when the sting has been removed with tweezers.

Travel sickness may sound like a minor problem but it can make travelling something of a trial for a dog's owner and, if it is not overcome, a travel-sick Shar Pei may end up staying behind at home instead of enjoying journeys with the family. You may find that a young puppy which suffers from this problem quickly outgrows it, especially if taken frequently on very short car journeys, then gradually building up the length of those journeys. There are some extremely good canine travel sickness tablets on the market from which there appear to be no side effects, so that they can be used safely, as long as you are careful never to overdose.

Dogs which have suffered from travel sickness, or have salivated excessively during travel, should be given a drink of water upon arrival at their destination.

Undescended testicles are always a cause for concern, for those which are retained can cause problems, such as a tumour. When neither testicle is descended the dog is known as a cryptorchid; if only one is descended he is a unilateral-cryptorchid. Technically the common term 'monorchid' should be applied only to dogs which actually possess only one testicle. The majority of cases of cryptorchidism and monorchidism are hereditary and breeding from such stock is definitely not to be recommended, though such dogs may be capable of reproducing.

CARING FOR THE ELDERLY SHAR PEI

If you are lucky, your Shar Pei will live to a ripe old age but, as with any breed, the older dog will need special care and attention and you may well see signs of the ageing process.

SPECIAL AREAS FOR ATTENTION

Your Shar Pei will stand the best chance of living a full and active life into old age if given plenty of exercise throughout life and not over-fed, so that, by the age of nine or ten, there are no problems with gross over-weight and inactivity. Excess weight puts strain on the heart, with premature death as the usual result.

On the other hand, the older dog should not be forced to take too much exercise; a short stroll, to keep up awareness of what is going on outside the immediate environment, will be sufficient, unless the dog is particularly active. Never walk your older Shar Pei too far from home, so that

Your responsibility as an owner starts from the first moment your puppy arrives home.

Photo: Colleen Kehe

you cannot get back quickly when you realise that tiredness is creeping on. Take especial care in hot weather that your dog is not over-exerted. Should there be any discomfort from the heat, a cool sponge bath will usually help to restore normal body temperature.

Because your Shar Pei is now less active, you will probably find that food intake will need to be reduced somewhat, probably by ten or twenty per cent. However, you may decide to increase the protein by giving more meat and less bulk. On the other hand, some older dogs have special dietary requirements and, in some cases, a diet which is lower in protein than normal can be the most appropriate. The latter is something which may have been recommended by your vet should

The days of glory when a dog is in the prime of life. However, the older Shar Pei deserves special attention, and this should be given throughout the last years.

Photo courtesy: Shirley Rafferty.

your Shar Pei have health problems in later life, so do please take his advice.

As I have said earlier in this book, the most suitable sleeping accommodation is that which is raised from the ground to eliminate draughts, and this is even more important as your Shar Pei gets older. Be sure that the bed is not so high that your old dog, who may by now be suffering from arthritis or aching joints, to a greater or lesser extent, has difficulty getting in and out. You will also have to watch your older dog if stair climbing is allowed. Your vet may be able to prescribe something to alleviate any pain, even something as simple as quarter or half an aspirin, or possibly extra vitamins. Massaging the legs can also help to keep the limbs as free-moving as possible, and a little gentle exercise, if only about the house and garden, should be encouraged so that the joints do not stiffen totally.

Hopefully you will have trained your Shar Pei, when young, to react properly to dental care, so the teeth will have been correctly cared for and you will be aware of any sudden change or discomfort. Strangely, a broken tooth does not always give the pain which we would associate with a human's tooth, but it will need to be checked by your vet. Personally I prefer to avoid anaesthetics for older dogs if at all possible but, if gums are diseased and teeth decayed, there may be no alternative. Again, this is something about which you will need to take advice from your vet and, if you have looked after your Shar Pei's teeth throughout the earlier years, you stand less chance of having to make a difficult decision for the comfort of your dog. Abscesses on the gums can sometimes go undetected until such time as a wound appears on the cheek or else the dog goes off food; immediate veterinary attention is a must, as such poison can get into the system and create even more problems.

Eyesight and hearing in the older Shar Pei may become less acute than it was in years gone by, so your dog should be carefully supervised in strange places, or if there is traffic about. In such circumstances always use a lead, as your dog may simply not hear or see danger approaching. If eyesight is beginning to fail, it will be helpful for your dog if furniture can remain more or less in the same place, to avoid accidents, and in case there is difficulty in hearing, don't get angry if there is no immediate reponse when you call – your Shar Pei may simply not have heard. I never like to take one of my older dogs by surprise and often I think they appreciate it if they can see the owner of the voice which is calling them. I find, also, that my older dogs seem to sleep very deeply and I try to avoid waking them suddenly, especially if they have a heart problem.

Be sure to regularly check the ears for a build-up of wax, for this, too, will add to hearing problems, and remember that, if your Shar Pei is not taking as much exercise on hard surfaces as before, nails will most probably grow rather too long. For this reason nails should be checked and trimmed regularly, if necessary. The coat of an older Shar Pei may also become thinner, so do keep your dog reasonably warm at all times and, if necessary, put on a suitable coat if walking outside in the winter months – your Shar Pei is unlikely to object to this new attire and will appreciate the warmth it gives.

Make sure that plenty of water is always available, as age may bring with it a slightly increased requirement for liquid intake, something which is quite normal. However, should your Shar Pei seem to be drinking excessively, this could be a sign that something is not working well inside the body. Naturally, if you are at all concerned that your Shar Pei seems to be going downhill fast, a visit to the vet is in order in an effort to alleviate the problem. It is surprising how many old dogs seem to live happy and comfortable lives almost to the end of their days.

FINAL PARTING

Sadly, sooner or later, the time will come when you have to part. The decision may be taken for you by natural causes or you may be put in that terrible dilemma of whether or not it would be kinder to have your Shar Pei peacefully put to sleep. If you feel that this decision is best, you may decide that you would like the vet to visit you at home, rather than take your dog along to the surgery. A great deal will depend on the relationship your dog has with the vet and on feeling comfortable in the surgery.

The injection given usually has fast results and your dog will simply go peacefully to sleep. Again, speaking from a personal viewpoint, I always like to stay with my own dogs until the very end – I feel I owe it to them. However, if you feel that you will get too upset, this may not be a good idea, for your dog will be aware of your emotions. On the other hand, if you feel that you, or another member of your family with whom the dog has a good rapport, are strong enough to control emotions until the end has come, I honestly feel this is better. There will be plenty of time for tears later.

Everyone has individual ideas concerning what should happen after a dog has died. There are several options. I always have my dogs cremated individually at a pet cemetery, something about which your vet will be able to advise you. If the dog has died in the surgery, your vet will be able to organise this for you or, if the death has taken place at home, you may have to call the cremation service yourself. Depending on the area in which you live, arrangements may vary but, usually, ashes can either be returned to you or can be scattered or buried at the cemetery. Such a service does, of course, cost money, but if you would be content for your dog to be cremated along with others the cost is somewhat reduced. The alternative is to let your vet take total care of the disposal, but this is not something I recommend. Personally, I like to know where my dogs have finally been laid to rest.

APPENDIX

SELECTED BIBLIOGRAPHY

Ash, Edward C: Dogs and Their History, Vol 2: Ernest Benn, 1927.

Ash, Edward C: This Doggie Business: Hutchinson & Co., 1934.

Carmello and Battagalia, Dr and L: Dog Genetics – How to Breed Better Dogs: T.F.H. Publications, 1978.

Collier, W F: Dogs of China and Japan in Nature and in Art: Heinemann, 1921.

Croxton Smith, A: Dogs Since 1900, Non-Sporting Breeds – Some Far Eastern Dogs: Andrew Dakers, 1950.

Cunliffe, Juliette: All About the Lhasa Apso: Pelham, 1990.

Cunliffe, Juliette: The Complete Shih Tzu: Ringpress Books, 1992.

Dale-Green, Patricia: Dog: Rupert Hart-Davis, 1966.

Dixey, Annie Coath: The Lion Dog of Peking: Latimer Trend & Co, 1931.

Frankling, Eleanor (Revised by Trevor Turner BVet. Med. MRCVS): Practical Dog Breeding and Genetics: Popular Dogs, 1981.

Gannon, Dee: The Complete Shar Pei: Howell Book House, Macmillan Publishing Company, 1988.

Godden, Rumer: The Butterfly Lions, The Pekingese in History, Legend and Art: Macmillan London Limited, 1977.

Graham Weall, Susan: The Pug: Popular Dogs, 1971.

Juliano, Annette: Treasures of China: Allen Lane, Penguin Books Ltd, 1981.

McDonald Brearley, Joan: The Book of the Shar-Pei: T.F.H. Publications, 1991.

Redditt, Jo Ann Thrower: Understanding the Chinese Shar Pei: Orient Publications, Inc., 1989.

Richards, Dr Herbert: Dog Breeding for Professionals: T.F.H. Publications, 1978.

Shaw, Vero: The Illustrated Book of the Dog: Cassell, Petter, Galpin & Co., 1881.

Sloan and Farquhar, A and A: Dog and Man, The Story of a Friendship: George H. Doran Company, 1925.

Spira, Harold R:Canine Terminology: David & Charles, 1982.
Turner, Trevor (BVet. Med. MRCVS): Veterinary Notes for Dog Owners: Popular Dogs, 1990.
Weathers Debo, Ellen: The Chinese Shar-Pei: T.F.H. Publications, 1986.
West, Geoffrey (MRCVS): All About Your Dog's Health: Pelham Books, 1979.
White, Kay: Dogs, Their Mating, Whelping and Weaning: K & R Books Ltd, 1977.
Wynyard, Ann Lindsay: Dog Directory Guide to Owning a Tibetan Spaniel: The Dog Directory, 1980.
McHennnan, Bardi. Dogs and Kids: Howell Book House, 1994.

OTHER PUBLICATIONS

Catalogues of Fine Oriental Ceramics and Works of Art, and Fine Chinese Export Porcelain and Jade Carvings - Sotheby & Co.
Chinese Art: Mount Trust Collection.

Simply Shar Pei - Midland Shar Pei Club (Proposed).
The Barker - Chinese Shar Pei Club of America.
The Wrinkle - The Shar Pei Club of GB.

VIDEOS
THE AKC BREED STANDARD SERIES
The Chinese Shar Pei

ADDITIONAL PROGRAMMES
General Interest:

In The Ring With Mr Wrong
AKC and the Sport of Dogs
The Quest for a Quality Show Dog
Gait: Observing Dogs in Motion
Dogsteps - A Study of Canine Structure and Movement by Rachel Page Elliot.

Available from:
AKC Videos,
5580 Centreview Drive, Suite 200
Raleigh, NC 27606 3390

SOME USEFUL ADDRESSES

KENNEL CLUBS

American K.C
51 Madison Avenue
New York
NY10010
Tel: (919) 233 9767
Fax: (212) 696 8299

English K.C.
1 Clarges Street
London W1Y 8AB, UK.
Tel: 071 493 6651
Fax:

Canadian K.C.
89 Skyway Ave
Etobicoke
Ontario
M9W 6R4
Tel: (416) 675 5511
Fax: (416) 675 6506

RESCUE SERVICE
Chinese Shar Pei Club of America
Alice Lawlor
Tel: (908) 295 7574
New Jersey

CHRONOLOGY OF CHINA

QIN DYNASTY 221 – 206 BC

HAN DYNASTY 206 BC – AD 220

Western Han 206 BC – AD 8

Interregnum AD 9 – 23

Eastern Han AD 25 – 220

SIX DYNASTIES AD 220 – 589

SUI DYNASTY AD 589 – 618

TANG DYNASTY AD 618 – 906

FIVE DYNASTIES AD 906 – 960

SONG DYNASTY AD 960 – 1279

YUAN DYNASTY (Mongols) AD 1260 – 1368

MING DYNASTY AD 1368 – 1644

QING DYNASTY (Manchus) AD 1644 – 1912

REPUBLIC AD 1928 – 1949

PEOPLE'S REPUBLIC AD 1949 –